BY THE EDITORS OF CONSUMER GUIDE®

FAVORITE BRAND NAME RECIPES

Salads of All Kinds

P. I. L.

Contents

Louis Weber, President
Publications International, Ltd.
3841 West Oakton Street
Skokie, Illinois 60076

Printed and bound by Pomurski tisk, Yugoslavia

10 9 8 7 6 5 4 3 2 1

Library of Congress Catalog Card Number: 82-82135
ISBN: 0-88176-236-9

Front Cover
Top row from left:
Chicken Salad Ambrosia (Campbell Soup Co.)
California Fruit Salad Rose (Thomas J. Lipton, Inc.)
Bottom row from left:
Fruited Chicken Salad (The Pillsbury Co.)
Lima Garlic Salad (Pepperidge Farm, Inc.)
Back Cover
Top row from left:
Wyler's® Taco Salad (Borden Inc.)
Vegetable Pepperoni Salad (Stokely-Van Camp, Inc.)
Bottom row from left:
Insalada Pepperidge (Pepperidge Farm, Inc.)
Sun World® Summer Salad (Sun World, Inc.)

Cover Design: Phyllis Ritthaler

Introduction

We have hundreds of **SALADS OF ALL KINDS** . . . Main Dish Salads that include **Seafood, Poultry, Meat** and luscious **Pasta**; Side Dish Salads like **Potato, Rice** and **Bean**; crispy green **Vegetable Salads**, refreshing **Vegetable & Fruit Combos**; delightful **Fruit** and beautiful **Gelatin Salads**. Salads for parties, picnics, lunches and dinners, and **Salad Dressings** for every taste. Use your leftover turkey or chicken in the ''Chicken Chow Mein Salad.'' If you have never made a Taco Salad, try any of the four recipes included in this book for a real taste treat. Everyone loves Macaroni Salad, and we have included a wide variety, so try a new recipe tonight. Instead of a hot vegetable course, surprise your family with cold ''Grecian Green Beans.'' For a new taste treat, try the wonderful ''Tangy Tangerine Coleslaw,'' or on a cold day, the ''Hot Cabbage Slaw'' hits the spot. For guests, set up a buffet of the ''Salad Antipasto'' or the ''Hearty Dilled Beefeater's Salad.''

You, the consumer, made this recipe collection possible by taking certain recipes that first appeared on food product labels or in advertisements and choosing them as your favorites! We have included only quality recipes that are or will soon become family treasures. The recipes are reprinted exactly as they appear on the labels or in the advertisements.

For the convenience of our readers we have included an address directory of all food manufacturers listed in the book (see **ACKNOWLEDGMENTS**). Any questions or comments regarding the recipes should be directed to the individual manufacturers for prompt attention. All recipes in this book have been copyrighted by the food manufacturers and cannot be reprinted without their permission. By printing these recipes, CONSUMER GUIDE® is *not* endorsing particular brand name foods.

Seafood Salads

Acapulco Shrimp Salad

1 (6 oz.) package **WAKEFIELD® Shrimp**
1½ cups sliced celery
2 medium tomatoes, sliced into wedges
¼ cup chopped green onion
3 tablespoons chopped sweet pickle
¾ cup kidney beans (optional)
½ cup shredded sharp Cheddar cheese
Ripe olives
Romaine or other salad greens
Thousand Island dressing

Thaw shrimp, drain and separate. Mix together celery, tomatoes, green onion, sweet pickle, kidney beans and Cheddar cheese. To serve salad, arrange crisp salad greens on four salad plates. Mound about ½ cup of shredded lettuce in center of each plate. Divide salad mixture equally over lettuce and top with shrimp. Garnish with ripe olives; serve with Thousand Island dressing.

Serves 4

RAGÚ
Spicy Shrimp Salad

1 pound medium shrimp, shelled and deveined
1 cup sour cream
¼ cup **RAGÚ® Spaghetti Sauce**
1½ teaspoons lemon juice
1 teaspoon grated onion
1 teaspoon horseradish
½ teaspoon Worcestershire sauce
TABASCO® Sauce
Salt, to taste
Pepper, to taste

In a large saucepan, bring 1 quart of water to a boil. Add shrimp, simmer 2-4 minutes or until shrimp turns pink; drain and chill. Combine remaining ingredients, cover and chill. To serve, toss shrimp with dressing. Spoon over shredded lettuce and garnish with lemon slices.

Serves about 4

It's a Mad Shrimp Salad

1 can (4½ ounces) **LOUISIANA BRAND Shrimp**
1 can (8 ounces or 1 cup) cut green beans
1 can (7 ounces or about 1 cup) whole kernel corn
1 cup sliced celery
3 green onions, chopped
1 medium-size tart red apple, unpeeled, diced
2 cups chopped crisp lettuce
½ cup any favorite oil and vinegar dressing

Have main ingredients well chilled. Drain shrimp and canned vegetables; combine and toss with celery, onion, apple, lettuce, and salad dressing.

4 generous servings

Best Foods.
HELLMANN'S.
Savory Shrimp Salad

1 cup **BEST FOODS®/HELLMANN'S® Real Mayonnaise**
½ cup chopped green onions
½ cup chopped parsley
2 tablespoons lemon juice
1 teaspoon sugar
¼ teaspoon salt
1 pound shrimp, cooked, cleaned, chilled

In small bowl stir together first 6 ingredients. Cover; chill at least 2 hours. Serve shrimp and dressing on avocado and tomato wedges. Garnish with lemon slices.

Makes 4 servings

Lime Seafood Louis

1½ cups mayonnaise
¼ cup catsup
2 tablespoons fresh Florida lime juice
1 teaspoon dried shredded green onion
Dash pepper
3 cups cooked shrimp or crab
Salad greens
Lime wedges

In medium bowl, blend mayonnaise, catsup, lime juice, onion and pepper. Chill. At serving time, arrange seafood on greens. Top with dressing. Garnish with wedges of lime.

Makes 6 servings (about 2 cups dressing)

Favorite recipe from the **Florida Lime Administrative Committee**

Shrimp Salad Polynesian

1 lb. **ATALANTA Frozen Shrimp**, Cooked, peeled, deveined
1 large, red apple, cored and cubed
1½ cups pineapple chunks
½ lb. grapes, green, seedless
1 cup yogurt, plain
1 Tbsp. curry powder
3 Tbsp. lemon juice
Lettuce leaves, Bibb or Romaine, as needed

Combine yogurt, curry powder and lemon juice. Mix well. Combine Shrimp, cubed apple, pineapple chunks and grapes. Toss gently with yogurt dressing. Serve on lettuce leaves.

Fisherman's Favorite Cioppino Salad

1 cup **WISH-BONE® Italian Dressing**
¼ cup dry white wine
¼ teaspoon dry basil or ¾ teaspoon chopped fresh basil
2 cups cooked Dungeness crabmeat (about ¾ lb.)
¾ pound large shrimp, cleaned and cooked
2 quarts mixed salad greens
3 cups coarsely chopped tomatoes
10 artichoke hearts, halved*
1 medium red onion, cut into rings

In large shallow baking dish, blend **WISH-BONE® Italian Dressing**, wine and basil; add crabmeat and shrimp. Cover and marinate in refrigerator, turning occasionally, at least 2 hours.

Meanwhile, in salad bowl, arrange salad greens, tomatoes, artichoke hearts and onion; chill. Just before serving, add seafood with marinade and toss. Garnish, if desired, with chopped parsley.

Makes 6 to 8 servings

*Substitution: Use 1 can (15 oz.) artichoke hearts, drained and halved.

Palm Beach Salad

1-12 ounce bag **BOOTH Peeled and Deveined Shrimp**
⅓ cup mayonnaise
⅓ cup heavy cream, whipped
½ cup mandarin orange sections
3 tablespoons chopped nuts
3 tablespoons coconut
2-3 drops **TABASCO® Sauce**
¼ teaspoon salt
Lettuce leaves

Boil shrimp according to package instructions. Drain, rinse and chill. Combine the rest of the ingredients except lettuce leaves thoroughly. Fold in shrimp. Chill for one hour. Serve on lettuce leaves.

Drambuie® Crabmeat Delight

1 cup flaked crabmeat (1 6½-oz. can or 1 6-oz. frozen package)
2 large canned artichoke hearts, chopped
2 hard cooked eggs, chopped
¼ cup thinly sliced small mushrooms
¼ cup sliced black olives
¼ cup mayonnaise
2 Tbsp. **DRAMBUIE®** liqueur
Snipped chives
Salt and pepper

Combine all ingredients, adding chives, salt and pepper to taste. Refrigerate until serving time. Serve on lettuce leaf with lemon wedges.

Two servings

Far East Crab Salad

6 to 8 ounces **ALASKA King Crab Meat**, thawed if necessary
½ cup sliced celery
⅓ cup *each* diced green pepper and sliced water chestnuts
1 can (13¼ oz.) pineapple chunks, drained
¼ cup toasted slivered almonds
½ cup mayonnaise
2 teaspoons lemon juice
½ teaspoon curry powder
Lettuce
1 avocado, peeled and sliced

Drain and slice crab. Combine crab with remaining ingredients except lettuce and avocado. Arrange crab mixture on lettuce-lined plates; garnish with avocado slices.

Makes 4 servings

Favorite recipe from the **Alaska Seafood Marketing Institute**

Aloha Crab Salad

1 (6-oz.) pkg. **WAKEFIELD®** Crabmeat
1 fresh pineapple
1 ripe avocado
1 tablespoon lemon juice
⅓ cup sliced water chestnuts
1 finely chopped green onion
1 cup mayonnaise
¼ teaspoon curry powder

Thaw crabmeat, drain and separate into chunks. Halve pineapple lengthwise and remove core; scoop out fruit and cut into chunks. Peel avocado and coarsely dice; sprinkle with lemon juice. Toss together pineapple chunks, water chestnuts, avocado, green onion and crabmeat. Spoon into pineapple shells and garnish with mayonnaise seasoned with curry. *Serves 4 to 5*

Mushroom-Clam Dinner Salad

½ cup **DIET SHASTA®** Orange
½ teaspoon minced garlic
1 tablespoon vinegar
1 teaspoon celery salt
⅛ teaspoon white pepper
1 teaspoon basil leaves, crushed
½ teaspoon thyme leaves, crushed
1 (6½ oz.) can minced clams, drained
1 cup finely chopped fresh mushrooms
¼ cup chopped green pepper
4 medium or small tomatoes
Crisp lettuce

Combine **DIET SHASTA®** with garlic, vinegar, salt, pepper, basil and thyme. Simmer about 5 minutes until liquid is reduced to about ¼ cup. Pour over drained clams and mushrooms. Chill several hours or overnight. Add green pepper. Cut tomatoes partially through to open like flowers. Arrange on crisp lettuce and spoon mushroom-clam mixture over each.

Makes 4 servings

Italian Scallop Salad

¾ pound cooked scallops, fresh or frozen
1 can (16 ounces) cut green beans, drained
2 hard-cooked eggs, chopped
⅔ cup sliced celery
⅓ cup raw cauliflower "Flowerettes"
⅓ cup thinly sliced unpeeled cucumber
¼ cup sliced green pepper
1 teaspoon salt
½ teaspoon pepper
½ cup Italian salad dressing
¼ cup chopped pimiento (Optional)
Radish roses
Salad greens

Remove any remaining shell from cooked scallops. Cut large scallops in half. Combine all ingredients except radish roses and salad greens; toss lightly. Place about one cup salad on each salad plate which has been lined with salad greens. Garnish with radish roses. *Serves 6*

Favorite recipe from the **National Marine Fisheries Service**

Tossed Fish Salad*

2½ cups water
¼ cup plus 1 teaspoon **LEA & PERRINS Worcestershire Sauce**, divided
2 tablespoons lemon juice
4 teaspoons onion powder
1½ teaspoons salt, divided
2 pounds cod or halibut fillets
1 cup cherry tomatoes, halved
1 cup thinly sliced celery
4 hard-cooked eggs, diced
½ cup mayonnaise
1 tablespoon sweet pickle relish
½ teaspoon garlic powder

In a medium skillet combine water, ¼ cup of the **LEA & PERRINS**, lemon juice, onion powder and 1 teaspoon of the salt. Bring to boiling point. Add fish. Reduce heat and simmer 12 to 15 minutes or just until fish flakes. Cool fish in liquid. Drain, flake and chill. In a salad bowl combine flaked fish, tomatoes, celery and eggs. Mix mayonnaise, relish and garlic powder with remaining 1 teaspoon **LEA & PERRINS** and ½ teaspoon salt. Spoon into fish mixture; toss gently. Serve on crisp lettuce, or in avocado halves, if desired. *Yield: 6 to 8 portions*

*May be prepared in advance of serving.

Fish Salad Veronique

¾ pound cooked tilefish, cut into 1-inch cubes
1 cup fresh pineapple chunks **OR** 1 can (5¼ ounces) pineapple chunks in natural juice, drained (reserving ¼ cup juice)
1 cup fresh orange segments, drained (reserving ¼ cup juice), seeded and membrane removed
1 cup seedless grapes
1 small red apple, unpared, cored and cut into 1-inch chunks
1 teaspoon lemon juice
½ teaspoon cornstarch **OR** arrowroot
¼ cup raisins
1 fresh pineapple shell **OR** Lettuce Leaves

Thaw fish if frozen. In a 2-quart mixing bowl, combine fish, pineapple, orange segments, grapes and apple. Cover and chill. Place reserved pineapple, orange and lemon juices in a 1-quart saucepan. Bring to a gentle boil and carefully stir in cornstarch. Cook until thickened, stirring constantly. Remove from heat and stir in ¼ cup raisins; cool. Serve in ¼ fresh pineapple shell or on a bed of lettuce. Spoon 1 tablespoon raisin dressing over each serving. *Makes 4 servings*

Favorite recipe from the **Florida Department of Natural Resources**

Popeye Salad With Farm-Raised Catfish

2 pounds **FARM-RAISED CATFISH Fillets**, fresh or frozen
1 teaspoon salt
1 large avocado, peeled and sliced into rings
1 tablespoon orange juice
1 pound fresh spinach, washed and torn into pieces
3 oranges, peeled and sectioned
1 can (5 ounces) water chestnuts, sliced
3 strips bacon, cooked, drained and crumbled
Salad Dressing*

Thaw fish if frozen. Sprinkle with salt. Place fish in a well-greased steamer pan and cook over boiling water for 10 to 12 minutes or until fish flakes easily when tested with a fork. Remove fish; cool and break into small pieces. Sprinkle avocado with orange juice. Combine fish, avocado, spinach, and orange sections in a large salad bowl. Toss with dressing. Sprinkle with water chestnuts and bacon. *Makes 6 servings*

*Salad Dressing

⅔ cup salad oil
⅓ cup orange juice
2 tablespoons sugar
1 tablespoon white distilled vinegar
½ teaspoon grated orange rind
½ teaspoon liquid hot pepper sauce
¼ teaspoon salt
¼ teaspoon dry mustard

Combine all ingredients and mix thoroughly. Chill.
Makes approximately 1 cup dressing

Prize winning recipe from the **Catfish Farmers of America**

Old Europe-Herring Hausfrauen Art

6 marinated herring fillets or 2 jars (8 oz. each) marinated herring pieces
2 cups thinly sliced, peeled apple
½ cup sliced onion
¼ cup sliced garlic dill pickle
1 cup mayonnaise
¼ cup whipping cream
1 tablespoon lemon juice
1 teaspoon Worcestershire sauce
¼ teaspoon salt
Dash white pepper
12 medium size parslied potatoes

Drain herring and cut fillets into small pieces. Combine apple, onion, pickle, and herring. Combine remaining ingredients and mix thoroughly. Pour over herring and let stand in the refrigerator for several hours. Serve with parslied potatoes. *Makes 6 servings*

Favorite recipe from the **National Marine Fisheries Service**

Chicken of the Sea® Mediterranean Tuna Salad

½ cup olive oil
¼ cup lemon juice
½ teaspoon salt
¼ teaspoon oregano leaves, crushed
⅛ teaspoon ground pepper
1½ quarts torn salad greens
2 cucumbers, sliced
6 green onions, thinly sliced
8 radishes, sliced
16 pitted ripe olives
1 can (13 oz.) **CHICKEN OF THE SEA® Solid White (albacore) Tuna**, drained
3 tomatoes, quartered
2 cups (8 oz.) crumbled feta cheese

For dressing, combine oil, lemon juice, salt, oregano and pepper. Chill. In salad bowl combine greens, cucumbers, onions, radishes and olives. Just before serving pour dressing over greens. Toss. Add remaining ingredients. Toss lightly.

Makes 6-8 servings

Lindsay.

Mexican Hat Salad

¾ cup **LINDSAY® Chopped Ripe Olives**
2 (7 ounce) cans tuna, drained and flaked
1 cup chopped celery
1 small cucumber, seeded and chopped
2 tablespoons minced onion
½ cup mayonnaise
2 teaspoons lemon juice
½ teaspoon chili powder
¼ teaspoon salt
3 cups shredded lettuce
4 crisp fried tortillas
Cherry tomatoes
Pepper rings, thinly sliced

Combine chopped olives with tuna, celery, cucumber and onion. Mix together mayonnaise, lemon juice, chili powder and salt. Just before serving, combine tuna and mayonnaise mixtures. Place shredded lettuce on large platter. Arrange a circle of tortillas on lettuce. Mound salad mixture on tortillas. Top with Pitted Ripe Olives. Garnish and arrange cherry tomatoes, ripe olives, and pepper rings around edge. *Makes 4 servings*

Delhi Tuna Salad

2 cans (6½ or 7 ounces) **STAR-KIST® Tuna**, drained
½ cup raisins
½ cup chopped green pepper
½ cup dry-roasted peanuts
¼ cup flaked coconut
2 tablespoons chopped chutney

In large bowl, mix all ingredients. Serve with Curry Dressing*. Delicious as is, or in a half cantaloupe. *Yield: 4 servings*
(Continued)

*Curry Dressing

¼ cup yogurt
¼ cup mayonnaise
1 tablespoon lemon juice
1 teaspoon curry powder
2 tablespoons chopped onion
¼ teaspoon salt

In a small bowl, mix all ingredients. *Yield: ¾ cup*

Mediterranean Tuna Salad
(Low Calorie)

1 cup boiling water
½ cup bulgar wheat
1 cup shredded carrots
1 cup diced celery
1 can (6½ or 7 ounces) tuna in water, drained, flaked
½ teaspoon celery seed
½ teaspoon dried leaf dill or dried leaf mint, crushed
½ teaspoon salt
Dash pepper
1 medium-size zucchini, thinly sliced
1 cup cherry tomato halves
1 cup plain low-fat yogurt

In large bowl, pour boiling water over bulgar; allow to stand 1 hour or until all liquid is absorbed. Add carrots, celery, tuna, celery seed, dill, salt and pepper; mix well. Cover. Chill several hours. Drain tuna mixture of excess liquid; top with cherry tomato halves; spoon yogurt over all and mix gently. Arrange zucchini slices in a ring around edge of large platter. Mound the tuna mixture in the center of the zucchini ring. Garnish with a dollop of yogurt. *Yield: 4 servings*

Calories: 200 per serving

Favorite recipe from the **Tuna Research Foundation**

Salade Nicoise

1 package (10 ounces) frozen French-style green beans
2 heads Bibb or Boston lettuce, torn into bite-size pieces
2 tomatoes, cut in sixths
2 hard-cooked eggs, peeled and cut into fourths
1 can (about 7 ounces) chunk white tuna, drained
2 tablespoons sliced ripe olives, drained
BAC★OS® Imitation Bacon
French Dressing*

Cook beans as directed on package; drain. Cover and refrigerate until chilled. Place lettuce in salad bowl. Arrange beans, tomatoes and eggs around edge of salad. Mound tuna in center; sprinkle with olives and imitation bacon. Serve with French Dressing. *4 servings*

*French Dressing

½ cup olive oil, vegetable oil or combination
2 tablespoons vinegar
2 tablespoons lemon juice
½ teaspoon salt
¼ teaspoon dry mustard
¼ teaspoon paprika

Shake all ingredients in tightly covered container.

Star-Kist Tuna

California Tuna Fruit Salad Platter

2 cans (6½ or 7 ounces) **STAR-KIST®** Tuna, drained
1 small cantaloupe, pared and cut in wedges
1 avocado, peeled and cut in wedges
1 small pineapple, pared, cored, and cut in strips or chunks
2 large bananas, cut in chunks
1 can (1 pound, 14 ounces) whole unpeeled apricots, drained
Small cluster of grapes
Watercress or escarole
Pineapple-Lime Cream Dressing*

Break **STAR-KIST®** Tuna into large chunks and arrange with fruit on large platter. Garnish with watercress or escarole. Serve immediately with Pineapple-Lime Cream Dressing. *Yield: 6 to 8 servings*

*Pineapple-Lime Cream Dressing

¼ cup sugar
2 tablespoons cornstarch
½ teaspoon salt
¼ teaspoon curry powder
⅛ teaspoon ground ginger
1½ cups pineapple juice
4 egg yolks, slightly beaten
½ teaspoon grated lime rind
¼ cup lime juice
⅔ cup sour cream or yogurt
½ cup mayonnaise

In a saucepan, mix sugar, cornstarch, salt, curry powder, and ginger. Stir in pineapple juice. Cook, stirring constantly until mixture boils and thickens. Stir a small amount of hot mixture into egg yolks. Stir warmed egg yolks into sauce and cook over very low heat for 2 minutes, stirring constantly. Stir in remaining ingredients and chill. *Yield: 2 cups*

FINLANDIA
IMPORTED
SWISS CHEESE

Finnish Tuna Salad

2 cans (6½ ounces each) tuna, drained, flaked
1 cup julienne strips **FINLANDIA** Swiss
1 cup mayonnaise
2 tablespoons chopped green onions
1 tablespoon lemon juice
1 cup sliced celery
2 cups halved green grapes
2 cups fresh pineapple chunks
1 can (11 ounces) mandarin oranges, drained
Leaf lettuce

Combine all ingredients, except lettuce. Chill several hours. When ready to serve, line salad bowl with greens. Spoon in salad. If desired, garnish with sliced almonds.

Makes 6 to 8 servings

Cottage Tuna Salad
(Low Calorie/Low Fat)

1 can (6½ ounces) tuna, packed in water, drained
1 cup low-fat cottage cheese
¼ cup chopped celery
¼ cup chopped green onion
2 tablespoons chopped fresh parsley
1 tablespoon capers
¼ cup plain low-fat yogurt
1 tablespoon lemon juice
½ teaspoon dry mustard
1 packet SWEET 'N LOW®
¼ teaspoon freshly ground pepper
¼ teaspoon salt

In medium bowl, combine tuna, cottage cheese, celery, green onion, parsley, and capers. Mix remaining ingredients in separate bowl. Add to tuna mixture and mix thoroughly. Cover and chill.

Per Serving (½ cup): Calories: 115; Fat: 1g   *4 servings*

S&W® Tiki-Taco Salad

1 (13½ oz.) can S&W® Pineapple Chunks, drained
2 (6½ oz.) cans S&W® Chunk Light Fancy Tuna, well-drained
⅓ cup sliced S&W® Pitted Ripe Olives
⅓ cup diced green pepper
3 Tbsp. sliced green onion
½ cup cubed Cheddar cheese
2 cups coarsely shredded lettuce
¾ cup mayonnaise
2 Tbsp. hot taco sauce
2 cups taco-flavored corn chips
Cherry tomatoes for garnish

Combine drained pineapple, tuna, olives, green pepper, onion, cheese and lettuce in large salad bowl. Blend mayonnaise and taco sauce together to make dressing. Just before serving add corn chips to salad bowl and toss lightly with the dressing. Garnish with cherry tomatoes.
Serves 6

New York Health Salad

2 cans (6½ or 7 ounces each) tuna, drained
1 cup chopped, peeled tomato
¼ cup chopped green pepper
2 tablespoons sunflower seeds
¼ cup toasted nuts
¼ cup chopped parsley
Salad greens
Cottage Cheese Dressing*

In medium bowl, mix together all ingredients except salad greens. Turn into bowl, lined with salad greens, and serve with Cottage Cheese Dressing.
Yield: 4 servings
(Continued)

*Cottage Cheese Dressing

1 carrot, pared and cut in chunks
1 cup creamed cottage cheese
3 tablespoons milk
1 teaspoon dill seed
1 tablespoon mayonnaise
¼ teaspoon salt
1 teaspoon grated onion

Grate carrot in electric blender. Add cottage cheese and milk, cover and process at high speed until smooth. Turn mixture into medium bowl; stir in remaining ingredients. If blender is not available, press cottage cheese through a sieve into a bowl, shred carrot, and stir in remaining ingredients.   *Yield: 1¼ cups*

Favorite recipe from the **Tuna Research Foundation**

TABASCO®
Tuna Cracked Wheat Salad

2½ cups water
1 package (8 ounces) wheat pilaf mix
¼ cup lemon juice
¼ cup salad oil
2 cans (6½ or 7 ounces each) tuna in vegetable oil
1 cucumber, pared, seeded and diced
½ cup diced pared carrot
⅓ cup sliced scallions
¼ pound mushrooms, sliced
1 tomato, chopped
½ cup sliced pitted ripe olives
½ cup chopped parsley
½ teaspoon salt
½ teaspoon TABASCO® Pepper Sauce
Salad greens

In medium saucepan bring water to boil. Add pilaf mix, reduce heat, cover and simmer 15 minutes. Remove from heat; stir in lemon juice and oil. Let stand at room temperature until cool. Stir in remaining ingredients except salad greens. Cover and chill several hours. Turn into bowl lined with salad greens. Serve with Yogurt Dressing.*   *Yield: 6 to 8 servings*

*Yogurt Dressing

2 containers (8 ounces each) plain yogurt
⅛ teaspoon TABASCO® Pepper Sauce
4 teaspoons chopped fresh mint or ¼ teaspoon dried dill weed

In a small bowl mix together yogurt, **TABASCO®** and mint; chill.
Yield: 2 cups dressing

Salmon Vegetable Salad
(Low Calorie)

	Calories
1—15½ oz. can Pink DOUBLE Q Pink Salmon*	554
1½ cups finely shredded green cabbage	33
1½ cups finely shredded red cabbage	33
1 cup diced green pepper	32
1 cup shredded carrot	46

(Continued)

Dressing:
1 cup low calorie plain yogurt 61
1 tablespoon vinegar 2
½ teaspoon dry mustard . . . .
½ teaspoon celery seed . . . . ──
761

Drain salmon and separate into bite size pieces. Combine cabbage, green pepper and carrot and mound on four salad plates. Top with salmon. Combine salad dressing ingredients and spoon over salmon.   *Makes 4 servings*

Calories per serving = Approx. 190

*DEMING'S, GILLNETTERSBEST or **HUMPTY DUMPTY Salmon** may be substituted.

Baked South-of-the-Border Salad

1 can (15½ oz.) **BUMBLE BEE®** Alaska Sockeye Red Salmon
2 cups sliced celery
¾ cup dairy sour cream
¼ cup sliced green onion
3 tablespoons diced green chiles
½ teaspoon garlic powder
½ teaspoon salt
3 cups corn chips
Paprika
Avocado slices
Lemon slices

Drain salmon, reserving 2 tablespoons liquid. Break salmon into medium-size chunks. Combine celery, sour cream, onion, chiles, reserved salmon liquid, garlic powder and salt. Mix lightly with salmon and corn chips. Turn into shallow 1½ quart baking dish. Sprinkle lightly with paprika. Bake in a 375°F. oven 20 minutes, until thoroughly heated. Garnish with avocado and lemon slices.
Makes 4 to 5 servings

DEMING'S

Salmon Waldorf Salad

15½ oz. can **DEMING'S Red Sockeye Salmon***
½ cup walnut halves & pieces
1¼ cup Italian Dressing & Marinade

Drain salmon, separate into bite size pieces & combine with walnuts and dressing. Chill 1 hr.

To Serve:
2½ cups diced apple tossed with 1 Tbsp. lemon juice
2 cups thinly sliced celery
2 ripe avocados, cored, peeled and sliced
Apple, Green Grapes, Lettuce

On individual salad plates, attractively arrange diced apple, celery and avocado on bed of lettuce. Top with chilled salmon mixture and garnish with grapes and apple slices brushed with lemon juice.
Serves 5-6

*DOUBLE Q, GILLNETTERSBEST or **HUMPTY DUMPTY Salmon** may be substituted.

The Delicious Sardine Salad

2 cans **KING OSCAR Sardines,** drained
2 large **DELICIOUS Apples,** peeled, cored, chopped
2 large oranges, peeled and cut into bite-size pieces
1 large sweet Spanish onion, peeled and chopped
½ cup walnuts, chopped
½ cup sour cream
¼ cup lemon juice
1 tsp. chopped chives
Lettuce
Parsley

In large salad bowl, toss together sardines, apple, orange, onion, walnuts. Make dressing by mixing together sour cream, lemon juice, chives. Pour dressing over salad and toss gently. Serve on bed of lettuce and garnish with parsley.   *Serves 6*

Summertime Salad Marinade

Dressing:
½ cup **PLANTERS® Peanut Oil**
⅓ cup white wine vinegar
¼ cup **DRY SACK® Sherry**
1 tablespoon Dijon mustard
½ teaspoon tarragon leaves
¼ teaspoon salt
⅛ teaspoon ground black pepper

2 cups blanched sliced zucchini, chilled
1 pound medium shrimp, shelled, cooked and chilled
1½ cups shredded cooked chicken, chilled
½ cup thinly sliced onion
1 tablespoon **DROMEDARY Sliced Pimientos**
Crisp lettuce leaves

DRESSING:

Combine peanut oil, vinegar, **DRY SACK® Sherry,** mustard, tarragon, salt and pepper. Mix well. Divide prepared dressing into 3 separate bowls.

Place zucchini and shrimp in separate bowls with dressing. Combine chicken, onion and pimientos; place in 3rd bowl of dressing. Toss each combination well. Place bowls in refrigerator and marinate 30 minutes. Spoon individual salads onto lettuce leaves.
Serves: 6

Poultry Salads

BUTTERBALL®

Dieter's Turkey Citrus Salad

1 cup cubed roast **BUTTERBALL®** Turkey
1 cup fresh grapefruit sections
½ cup fresh orange sections
½ small head lettuce, broken into bite-size pieces
Low calorie dressing
4 leaves garden lettuce or endive

Toss together lightly turkey, fruit and lettuce with enough dressing to coat. Serve on lettuce leaves arranged on 2 salad plates.
Yield: 2 servings

9

Chicken Salad Ambrosia

¼ cup bottled Italian dressing
¼ cup orange juice
1 teaspoon honey
1 tablespoon toasted sesame seed
⅛ teaspoon grated orange rind
2 cans (5 ounces each) SWANSON Chunk Chicken
6 cups salad greens torn in bite-size pieces
1 cup sliced cucumber
½ cup sliced radishes
½ cup green pepper strips
½ cup orange sections cut-up
1 small red onion sliced

To make salad dressing, in bowl, combine bottled dressing, orange juice, honey, sesame seed and orange rind; chill. In large bowl, combine remaining ingredients. Serve with salad dressing.

Makes about 9 cups, 6 servings

Fruited Chicken Salad

10-oz. pkg. AMERICAN BEAUTY® Large
    SHEL-RONI®
1 cup mayonnaise
1 teaspoon salt
1 teaspoon dry mustard
½ teaspoon paprika
3 (5-oz.) cans boned chicken or 2 cups cubed, cooked
    chicken
2 cups melon balls or cubes
20-oz. can pineapple chunks, drained
⅓ cup sliced almonds, toasted

Cook shells to desired doneness as directed on package. Drain and rinse under cold water. In large bowl, combine mayonnaise, salt, mustard and paprika; stir until well blended. Fold in remaining ingredients, except almonds. Refrigerate 2 to 3 hours to blend flavors. Serve on lettuce leaves; sprinkle almonds over top before serving. *6 servings*

HIGH ALTITUDE—Above 3500 Feet: Cooking times may need to be increased slightly.

Chicken 'n' Grapefruit Salad

2 SUNKIST® Grapefruit, peeled, sectioned, drained
½ cup sliced celery
1 jar (2 oz.) sliced pimientos
2 cups cubed cooked chicken or turkey
⅔ cup mayonnaise or salad dressing
3 Tbsp. chopped green onions
2 tsp. prepared mustard
¼ tsp. salt
Crisp salad greens
12 ripe olives

Reserve 12 grapefruit sections for garnish. Cut remaining sections in half and combine in large bowl with remaining ingredients except salad greens and olives; chill. To serve, on 4 salad plates arrange greens; top with chicken mixture. Garnish with reserved grapefruit sections and olives.

Makes 4 servings (about 4 cups)

VARIATION:

Substitute 2 cans (about 7 oz. each) tuna, drained, chunked, for 2 cups chicken. Omit salt.

Molded Turkey Salad

2 envelopes unflavored gelatin
½ cup cold water
3 cups boiling water
3 HERB-OX® Chicken Bouillon Cubes or 1 tablespoon
    HERB-OX® Instant Chicken Style Bouillon
2 cups cooked turkey or chicken, chopped
1 onion, grated
⅓ cup chopped celery
1 tablespoon chopped parsley
2 tablespoons mayonnaise
2 tablespoons cream (any type)

Sprinkle gelatin on cold water, let stand 5 minutes. Add boiling water and bouillon cubes or instant bouillon, stir over low heat until gelatin is dissolved. Cool until aspic is thick and syrupy. Swirl enough thickened mixture in a chilled 5-cup pan or mold to coat bottom and sides. Chill until set. Combine remaining ingredients, blend well. Add ½ cup aspic, adjust seasoning. Fill aspic-lined pan smoothly, add remaining aspic. Chill until firm, unmold to serve. *Makes 4 to 6 servings*

Home Style Ruby Chicken Salad

3 medium TEXAS RUBY RED Grapefruit, chilled
1 broiler-fryer chicken (2 to 2½ lbs.) quartered or 2 cups
    cooked chicken
2 teaspoons salt
½ cup yogurt
¼ cup mayonnaise
⅛ to ¼ teaspoon dill weed
½ cup chopped celery
4 to 5 tablespoons chopped green onions
¼ cup ripe olives

In medium saucepan, place chicken, 1 teaspoon salt, and cover with water. Heat to boiling. Cover, reduce heat and simmer for 40 minutes. Remove chicken and cool slightly. When cool enough to handle, cut chicken into bite-size pieces. Discard bones and skin.

Meanwhile cut grapefruit in half crosswise; cut around each section to loosen from membrane or use serrated grapefruit spoon. Remove sections from shell and cut into bite-size pieces; drain well. Scrape remaining membrane from shells. Refrigerate until ready to use.

In medium bowl, combine yogurt, mayonnaise, 1 teaspoon salt and dill weed; stir well. Add grapefruit, chicken, and remaining ingredients; toss lightly. Spoon about ¾ cup chicken mixture into each grapefruit shell. Cover and chill until ready to serve.

6 servings

Favorite recipe from the **Texas Citrus Industry**

Brandied Chicken-Vegetable Salad

2 (10½ oz.) cans condensed chicken broth
2 envelopes plus 2 teaspoons unflavored gelatin
½ cup California Brandy
3 tablespoons white wine vinegar
½ teaspoon salt
3 drops TABASCO® Sauce
1 cup sliced yellow crook-neck squash
1 cup fresh or frozen peas
1 small avocado, sliced
1½ cups shredded cooked chicken
¼ cup diced pimiento
¼ cup sliced green onion
½ cup shredded carrot

Chill broth before opening cans, so any fat can be removed easily. Remove and discard fat. Sprinkle gelatin over ½ cup broth and let stand 5 minutes to soften. Heat remaining broth, add gelatin and stir until dissolved. Stir in brandy, vinegar, salt and TABASCO®. Cool until mixture begins to thicken slightly.

Meanwhile, cook squash about 5 minutes, until tender-crisp, and peas 5 to 10 minutes. Drain well, keeping separate.

When gelatin is cooled and lightly thickened, turn about ½ cup into oiled 6½ cup ring mold, and set in shallow pan of ice water. Arrange avocado slices around bottom and side of mold, and let stand until gelatin is set to hold in place. Mix about 1 cup of the gelatin mixture with chicken, pimiento and onion, and spoon into mold. Chill a few minutes, then add squash and about ½ cup more of the gelatin mixture. Chill again, and add peas and more gelatin, then carrots with remaining gelatin. Chill firm, at least 3 hours.

At serving time, unmold, and garnish with lettuce. Serve plain or with mayonnaise or dairy sour cream. *Makes 6 servings*

Note: For perfect layers, chill each until just set in pan with ice water before adding next layer.

Favorite recipe from the **California Brandy Advisory Board**

Satisfying Chicken Salad
(Low Calorie)

7 oz. package CREAMETTES® Macaroni (2 cups uncooked)
2 cups cooked chicken, diced
1 cup celery, diced
⅓ cup sweet pickles, chopped
2 tablespoons onion, chopped
2 tablespoons pimiento, diced
1 teaspoon salt
⅛ teaspoon dry mustard
Dash TABASCO® Sauce
½ cup low calorie mayonnaise
Lettuce
1 medium tomato, cut into 8 wedges

Prepare **CREAMETTES®** according to package directions for salad use. Drain. Combine macaroni, chicken, celery, sweet pickles, onion, pimiento, salt, dry mustard and **TABASCO®**. Toss with mayonnaise. Chill. Serve on lettuce. Garnish with tomato wedges. *4 servings*

Calories: Approximately 390 calories each

REALEMON
Tropical Chicken Salad

4 cups cooked cubed chicken or turkey
2 large oranges, peeled, sectioned and drained
1½ cups cut-up fresh pineapple, drained
1 cup seedless white grape halves
1 cup chopped celery
¾ cup mayonnaise or salad dressing
¼ cup REALEMON® Lemon Juice from Concentrate
1 teaspoon ground ginger
½ teaspoon salt
½ to ¾ cup cashew nuts

In large bowl, combine chicken, fruit and celery. Chill. In small bowl, combine remaining ingredients except cashews. Chill. Just before serving combine chicken mixture, dressing and nuts. Serve in hollowed out pineapple shells or on lettuce leaves. Refrigerate leftovers. *Makes about 2 quarts*

Tatra Ham and Chicken Salad

3 cups cut-up ATALANTA/KRAKUS/POLKA Polish Ham
2 cups cut-up cooked chicken
1 cup diagonally sliced celery
1 cup cubed fresh or canned pineapple
½ cup finely chopped green pepper
½ cup halved green grapes
2 teaspoons grated onion
¼ cup light cream
⅔ cup mayonnaise
1 teaspoon salt
Generous dash pepper
2 tablespoons lemon juice
Salad greens
Toasted slivered almonds

Combine ham, chicken, celery, pineapple, green pepper, grapes and onion. Blend cream into mayonnaise; stir in salt, pepper and lemon juice. Toss dressing with ham mixture. Refrigerate until ready to serve. To serve, arrange salad on greens and garnish with almonds. *Makes 6 to 8 servings*

Wyler's
Chicken Pineapple Salad

2 cups cubed cooked chicken
1 cup chopped celery
1 (8-ounce) can crushed pineapple packed in natural juice, drained
¼ cup plain yogurt
2 tablespoons chopped green onion
1 teaspoon WYLER'S® Chicken-Flavor Instant Bouillon
⅛ teaspoon ground nutmeg
OLD LONDON® Melba Toast or Rounds

In medium bowl, combine all ingredients except Melba Toast; mix well. Cover; chill thoroughly. Stir before serving. Serve with Melba Toast. Refrigerate leftovers. *Makes 4 cups*

Fiesta Chicken Salad

½ cup mayonnaise or salad dressing
1 tablespoon milk or cream
1 teaspoon lemon juice
¼ teaspoon nutmeg
⅛ teaspoon curry powder
2 whole cooked chicken breasts, diced into ½-inch cubes
1 can (30 ounces) **STOKELY'S FINEST®** Fruit Cocktail, chilled and drained
¼ cup toasted, slivered almonds

Blend together mayonnaise, milk, lemon juice, nutmeg, and curry powder. Fold in chicken and chill 30 minutes. When ready to serve, add fruit cocktail and almonds. Serve on bed of lettuce.

4 to 6 servings

Chicken Salad Supreme

3 5-oz. cans **BANQUET®** Boned Chicken, drained and cubed
1½ cups thinly sliced celery
3 Tbsp. lemon juice
1 cup seedless grapes
4 ripe olives, sliced
2 Tbsp. sliced pimiento
½ tsp. dry mustard
1 tsp. salt
¼ tsp. pepper
Dash ground allspice
2 tsp. capers
½ cup mayonnaise
½ cup toasted slivered almonds or nut meats
Endive
Black olives
Pimiento strips

Combine chicken, celery and lemon juice. Chill. Add grapes, olives and pimiento. Combine mustard, salt, pepper, allspice, capers and mayonnaise; add to chicken mixture. Toss lightly. Add almonds; toss again. Serve on beds of endive, garnished with olives and pimiento.

6-8 servings

Jiffy Summer Salad

1¼ cups creamed cottage cheese
1 can (4¾ ounces) **UNDERWOOD®** Chunky Chicken Spread
1 tablespoon chopped onion
1 teaspoon dried parsley flakes
8 slices canned pineapple rings
Lettuce leaves

In a large bowl, mix together cottage cheese, chunky chicken spread, onion and parsley. Arrange 2 pineapple rings per serving on a bed of lettuce. Scoop chicken salad mixture on top of pineapple. Chill.

Makes 4 servings

Tangy Chicken Salad

3 cups chopped cooked chicken
⅓ cup **B&B Liqueur**
2 cups halved seedless green grapes
1 cup sliced celery
⅓ cup chopped green pepper
1 can (8 oz.) chunk pineapple, drained
½ cup coarsely chopped walnuts
1 cup mayonnaise
Lettuce cups

Combine chicken and **B&B Liqueur** in a small deep bowl. Cover and chill 1 hour. In a large bowl combine chicken mixture, grapes, celery, green pepper, pineapple and walnuts. Toss thoroughly with mayonnaise. To serve lightly pile into individual lettuce cups.

Makes 6 servings

Best Foods® HELLMANN'S®

Orange Chicken Salad

½ cup **BEST FOODS®/HELLMANN's®** Real Mayonnaise
¼ cup thawed orange juice concentrate
½ teaspoon tarragon
½ teaspoon salt
⅛ teaspoon white pepper
2 cups cooked diced chicken
½ cup chopped celery
½ cup sliced water chestnuts

In medium bowl stir together **Real Mayonnaise**, orange juice concentrate, tarragon, salt and pepper. Add chicken, celery and water chestnuts; toss until well mixed. Cover and refrigerate.

Makes 3½ servings

Chicken Chow Mein Salad

1½ cups cubed cooked chicken
1 (16 oz.) can **VEG-ALL®** Mixed Vegetables, drained and chilled
6 hard-cooked eggs, sliced
1 cup diced celery
¼ cup coarsely chopped green pepper
¼ cup chopped pimiento
¾ cup real mayonnaise
2 Tbsp. minced onion
1 tsp. fresh lemon juice or to taste
½ tsp. salt or to taste
¼ tsp. freshly ground pepper
1 (5 oz.) can chow mein noodles

Garnish:
Green pepper strips
Pimiento strips

Combine chicken, **VEG-ALL®**, eggs, celery, green pepper, and pimiento; toss gently just to mix. Combine mayonnaise, onion, lemon juice, salt and pepper; blend into chicken mixture. Refrigerate. To serve, mound chicken salad in center of serving platter and surround with chow mein noodles. Garnish with additional strips of green pepper and pimiento.

Serves 4 to 6

Serendipity Salad

(Low Calorie)

1 can (5 ounces) **SWANSON Chunk White or Thigh Chicken**
2 cups salad greens torn in bite-size pieces
1 cup cauliflowerets
½ cup cherry tomatoes cut in half
1 small onion, sliced
⅓ cup bottled low-calorie Italian dressing

In bowl, combine all ingredients except dressing. Toss lightly with dressing. *Makes about 5 cups, 3 servings*

Calories: About 115 calories per serving.

Lindsay®

Chicken Salad Tarts

2½ cups diced cooked chicken
1 cup **LINDSAY® Pitted Ripe Olives**
¼ cup chopped celery
¼ cup chopped green pepper
2 tablespoons chopped pimiento
2 tablespoons sweet pickle relish
1 tablespoon finely minced onion
½ cup mayonnaise
½ teaspoon salt
⅛ teaspoon pepper

Quarter olives. Combine all ingredients and mix well. Use as filling for tiny baked tart shells. *Makes about 3 cups salad*

Wheat Germ Stuffed Tomato Salad

1 whole chicken breast, boned, skinned and diced
1 Tbsp. butter or margarine
4 large, firm, ripe tomatoes
¾ cup **KRETSCHMER Regular Wheat Germ**
⅓ cup chopped green onion
⅓ cup chopped green pepper
¾ tsp. curry powder
½ tsp. thyme leaves, crushed
½ tsp. salt
⅛ tsp. pepper

Sauté chicken in butter until tender (about 5 minutes). Cut thin slice from tops of tomatoes. Scoop out pulp, leaving shells intact. Dice tomato tops and pulp. Drain. Combine all ingredients *except* tomato shells. Mix well. Spoon mixture into shells. Serve on lettuce garnished with avocado wedges and ripe olives if desired. *Makes 4 servings*

Note: To serve hot, place in shallow baking pan and bake at 350° for about 25 minutes until hot. Top with yogurt if desired.

Turkey Hawaiian

3 whole fresh pineapples
2½ cups cooked cubed **JENNIE-O Turkey**
1 cup green seedless grapes
½ cup sliced celery
½ cup coarsely chopped nuts
1 can (8 oz.) Mandarin oranges, drained
1 cup dairy sour cream
¼ cup firmly packed brown sugar
Walnut halves, if desired

Cut pineapples in half. Remove fruit; cut into bite-size pieces. Combine pineapple pieces and remaining ingredients, except walnut halves. Spoon mixture into pineapple shells. Garnish with walnut halves, if desired. *6 servings*

Chicken Salad a la Tarragon

(Low Calorie)

2 cups diced cooked chicken
1 cup sliced celery
2 tablespoons finely chopped green pepper
1 tablespoon finely chopped green onion
2 teaspoons chopped pimiento
Salt
Crisp lettuce
Creamy Tarragon Dressing*

Combine chicken, celery, green pepper, onion and pimiento. Salt to taste. When ready to serve, spoon onto crisp lettuce on chilled salad plates. Pass Creamy Tarragon Dressing.

Makes 4 servings

Calories: 216 per serving

*Creamy Tarragon Dressing

Beat ¾ cup instant nonfat dry milk with ½ cup **DIET SHASTA® Ginger Ale** until fluffy. Crumble 1 chicken bouillon cube into ¼ cup tarragon flavor vinegar. Add to first mixture beating until thick. Add 1 teaspoon dry mustard, ½ teaspoon crumbled tarragon leaves, ¼ teaspoon paprika, 1 teaspoon onion powder, ½ teaspoon salt and 1 tablespoon chopped parsley. Stir to blend and serve at once. *Makes about 2 cups*

Calories: 43 per serving

Carl Buddig

Buddig Stuffed Tomato Salad

4 ripe tomatoes
Lettuce cups
1 package **BUDDIG Smoked Sliced Turkey** or **Chicken**, cut up
3 tablespoons sweet pickle relish
3 tablespoons finely chopped celery
Mayonnaise

Turn tomatoes stem end down; cut each not quite through in wedges; spread apart. Place in lettuce cups on serving plate. Combine **BUDDIG Turkey** or **Chicken**, pickle relish, celery and enough mayonnaise to moisten. Spoon into center of tomatoes.

Serves 4

Chinese Chicken Salad

1 broiler-fryer chicken
2 ribs celery
1 carrot
1 teaspoon salt
1 bay leaf
1 small onion
1 cup water
1 can (8½ oz.) water chestnuts, drained (1 cup)
1 can (8½ oz.) bamboo shoots (1 cup)
2 ribs celery, sliced
2 canned pimientos, chopped
2 green onions, thinly sliced
¾ cup **BEST FOODS®/HELLMAN'S®** Real
  Mayonnaise
2 tablespoons soy sauce
1 tablespoon lemon juice
1 quart torn lettuce pieces

Cook chicken with celery, carrot, salt, bay leaf, onion and water about 40 minutes or until tender. Cool; remove skin and bones and cut into bite-size pieces. Mix water chestnuts, bamboo shoots, sliced celery, pimiento, green onion and chicken. Toss lightly; cover and chill. Mix together **Real Mayonnaise**, soy sauce and lemon juice; chill. Just before serving toss chicken mixture with dressing. Serve salad on a bed of torn lettuce pieces.

Makes 4 to 6 servings

Note: If desired, serve dressing on the side instead of tossing with chicken mixture.

California Turkey Salad

Salad:
2 pounds **JENNIE-O Fully Cooked Turkey Breast,**
  cubed
1 cup sliced celery
1 cup sliced ripe olives
½ cup toasted slivered almonds
Leaf lettuce
3 small avocados, each cut into 12 slices*
4 medium oranges, peeled and sectioned
12 strawberries, halved
Green seedless grapes**

Dressing:
1½ cups vegetable oil
½ cup light wine or cider vinegar
3 tablespoons sugar
2 teaspoons each salt and minced parsley
½ teaspoon each dry mustard, basil, and pepper
1 garlic clove, minced

In medium bowl, combine all Dressing ingredients. Refrigerate at least one hour. Shake before serving. In large bowl, combine turkey, celery and olives. Assemble salads by lining six plates with lettuce, spooning on about one cup of turkey mixture and garnishing the top with slivered almonds and grapes. Surround salad with avocado slices, orange sections, strawberry halves and additional grapes or whole olives. Drizzle with Dressing.

Makes 6 salads

*Dip avocado slices in lemon juice to prevent discoloring.
**A combination of red and green grapes may be used.
You may substitute other **JENNIE-O** turkey products in this recipe.

Cookin' Good™ Pocket Sandwiches

2 cups of cooked, minced **COOKIN' GOOD™ Chicken**
8 slices of crisp, crumbled bacon
1-8 ounce container of sour cream
¼ cup mayonnaise
2 tablespoons minced onion
½ cup finely chopped celery (about 3-4 ribs)
½ cup black olives, sliced
½ teaspoon salt
½ teaspoon black pepper
¼ teaspoon poultry seasoning
2 tablespoons white wine or lemon juice

1 refrigerated can of biscuits (10-12 biscuits)
1 egg beaten

In a large mixing bowl combine mayonnaise, sour cream, celery, onion and spices, blend well after each addition. To this mixture add lemon juice, bacon and gradually add minced **COOKIN' GOOD™ Chicken** and olives. **Tip:** For ease in mincing **COOKIN' GOOD™ Chicken**, process in a blender or food processor according to manufacturers directions. Blend mixture well.

On a floured pastry sheet or board, using a floured rolling pin, roll each biscuit to a 4-5 inch circle. Place ¼ cup of chicken mixture on each circle, fold in half and crimp edges with a fork to seal. Place pocket sandwiches on an ungreased cookie sheet. Brush with beaten egg and prick tops of sandwiches with a fork once or twice to allow steam to escape. Bake 375° for 12-15 minutes or until golden brown. Remove to a cooling rack. May be frozen for one month, properly wrapped. This salad can also be eaten cold on any type of bread or on a bed of lettuce.

Serves 4-6

FOOD PROCESSOR METHOD:
To prepare this recipe in a food processor continue adding ingredients. Process 1 minute to blend all ingredients.

Lunchbox tip: Place one or two frozen sandwiches in lunchbox—will be ready to eat by lunch time!

Best Foods® HELLMANN'S®
Lemon-Ginger Chicken Salad

½ cup **BEST FOODS®/HELLMANN'S®** Real
  Mayonnaise
¼ cup dairy sour cream
1 tablespoon sugar
½ teaspoon grated lemon rind
1 tablespoon lemon juice
½ teaspoon ground ginger
¼ teaspoon salt
2 cups cooked cubed chicken
1 cup seedless green grapes
1 cup sliced celery

In large bowl stir together first 7 ingredients. Add chicken, grapes and celery; toss to coat well. Cover; chill at least 2 hours. Serve in cantaloupe halves; sprinkle with toasted slivered almonds. Garnish with lemon leaves and strawberries. *Makes 4 servings*

Teriyaki Slim 'n Trim Salad

(Low Calorie)

¼ pound fresh spinach
½ pound fresh apricots, halved and pitted
⅓ pound cooked white chicken, cut in pieces
⅓ pound lean roast beef, thinly sliced
⅓ cup sliced scallions, (cut in 1-inch pieces)
⅓ cup sliced celery
4 medium mushrooms, sliced
Paprika Dressing (recipe follows)
Oriental Dressing (recipe follows)

Arrange spinach, apricots, chicken, beef, scallions, celery and mushrooms in groups on large platter. Serve with Paprika Dressing and Oriental Dressing. *Makes 4 servings*

Calories: One serving: About 260 calories

Paprika Dressing

Combine ¼ teaspoon each dry mustard and paprika, ¾ teaspoon salt, 1 teaspoon sugar, 1 beaten egg, ¼ cup mild vinegar and 2 tablespoons olive or salad oil in top of double boiler. Cook, stirring constantly, over slowly boiling water until mixture thickens. Remove from heat and cool.

Oriental Dressing

Combine 2 tablespoons lemon juice, 2 tablespoons soy sauce, 2 teaspoons sugar and ½ teaspoon finely chopped crystallized ginger.

Favorite recipe from the **California Apricot Advisory Board**

German Chicken and Potato Salad

4 slices bacon
2 tablespoons flour
1 cup water
¼ cup wine vinegar
1 teaspoon sugar
⅛ teaspoon pepper
4 cups sliced cooked potatoes
2 cans (5 ounces each) **SWANSON Chunk White or Thigh Chicken**
¼ cup chopped green pepper
¼ cup chopped onion

In skillet, cook bacon until crisp; remove and crumble. Pour off all but ¼ cup drippings; blend in flour. Cook a few minutes, stirring constantly. Remove from heat. Add water, a little at a time, stirring until smooth after each addition. Add vinegar, sugar and pepper. Cook, stirring until thickened. Add bacon and remaining ingredients. Heat; stir occasionally.
Makes about 5 cups, 4 servings

Egg Salads

Continental Egg Salad

8 hard-cooked eggs,* chopped
½ cup chopped celery
½ cup shredded carrots
¼ cup mayonnaise or salad dressing
1 tablespoon chopped chives
½ teaspoon seasoned salt
6 tomatoes
Shredded carrots, optional
Chopped chives, optional

Combine eggs, celery, carrots, mayonnaise, chives and seasoned salt; mix until blended. Cut tomatoes in 6 sections almost to stem end; fill each with approximately ⅓ cup egg salad. Garnish with carrots and chives, if desired. *Makes 6 servings*

*Hard-Cooked Eggs

Cover EGGS in pan with enough WATER to come at least 1 inch above eggs. Cover; bring rapidly just to boiling. Turn off heat; if necessary remove pan from unit to prevent further boiling. Cover; let stand in hot water 15 minutes for large eggs—adjust time up or down accordingly for other sizes. Cool eggs immediately and thoroughly in cold water—shells are easier to remove and dark surface is prevented on yolks. To remove shell: Crackle shell by tapping gently all over. Roll egg between hands to loosen shell; then peel, starting at large end. Holding egg under running cold water or dipping in bowl of water helps to ease off shell.

Favorite recipe from the **American Egg Board**

Confetti Egg Salad

4 hard-cooked eggs, diced
¼ cup mayonnaise
2 tablespoons diced green pepper
2 tablespoons diced pimiento
2 teaspoons **LEA & PERRINS Worcestershire Sauce**

Combine all ingredients. Chill. *2 servings*

Meat Salads

Ham and Pea Stuffed Tomatoes

¼ cup mayonnaise, or salad dressing
½ teaspoon prepared mustard
⅛ teaspoon pepper
1 cup cold cooked peas
1 cup diced **WILSON® Ham**
2 green onions, sliced
4 medium tomatoes

Combine mayonnaise, mustard and pepper in medium bowl. Add peas, ham and green onion. Chill at least 1 hour. Slice top third off tomatoes. Scoop out center pulp and seeds. Chill tomato cups. To serve, spoon ham salad into tomatoes. *Makes 4 servings*

Sausage-Avocado Salad

2 Avocados, peeled and cut in quarters
Filling:
¼ lb. Pepperloaf (Diced)
¼ lb. Mortadella (Diced)
¼ lb. Chicken Loaf (Diced)
¼ lb. Summer Sausage (Diced)
1 cup mayonnaise
½ teaspoon mustard
Garnish:
4 teaspoons mayonnaise
8 black olive slices
4 cherry tomatoes
8 sprigs parsley

Combine filling ingredients and divide on quartered avocado spears. Garnish each spear with a half teaspoon mayonnaise, ½ cherry tomato, 2 olive slices and a sprig of parsley.

Serves 8

Favorite recipe from the **National Hot Dog Council**

Ham Stuffed Avocados

½ cup mayonnaise or salad dressing
2 tablespoons catsup or chili sauce
1 tablespoon vinegar
⅛ teaspoon garlic salt
1½ cups diced **WILSON® Ham**
½ cup thinly sliced celery
¼ cup chopped green pepper
1 hard cooked egg, chopped
2 avocados

To make dressing, combine mayonnaise, catsup, vinegar and garlic salt. In another bowl, combine ham, celery, green pepper and egg. Stir in 2 tablespoons of the dressing. Chill at least 1 hour. Cut avocados in half and remove pit. Spoon about ½ cup ham mixture into each cavity. Serve remaining dressing with the avocados.

Makes 4 servings

Mandarin Salad

¼ cup French dressing
1 teaspoon **LA CHOY® Soy Sauce**
2 cups diced cooked ham or veal
1 can (1 lb.) **LA CHOY® Fancy Bean Sprouts**, drained
¼ cup chopped onion
½ cup chopped sweet pickle
1 teaspoon salt
Dash pepper
¼ teaspoon monosodium glutamate desirable
¾ cup mayonnaise

Combine French dressing and Soy Sauce. Marinate meat in mixture for 30 minutes. Chill. Add remaining ingredients; mix lightly. Serve on crisp salad greens.

Yield: 4 Servings

Bacon Cheese Salad

3 or 4 hard cooked eggs
6 to 8 slices bacon
1 head lettuce
3 or 4 green onions
1 slice dry toast
1 clove garlic, cut in half
2 cups **SEALTEST® Cottage Cheese**
French Dressing to taste

Peel, then chop eggs coarsely. Fry bacon until crisp, drain on paper and crumble coarsely.

Tear lettuce into bite-size pieces. Chop green onions. Rub toast on both sides with a clove of garlic. Cut into small cubes. Place croutons in the bottom of a salad bowl. Then add lettuce and sprinkle with onions. Cover and refrigerate until ready to serve.

To serve, toss lettuce mixture with French Dressing. Spread cottage cheese on top and sprinkle with crumbled bacon and eggs.

6 servings

California Salad

1 small head iceburg lettuce
½ head romaine lettuce
4 **VIENNA® Franks**, cut crosswise
4 slices Swiss cheese, cut in julienne strips
2 green onions, chopped
1 small can ripe olives, cut crosswise
1 large tomato, cut in wedges
Croutons

Break lettuce into bite-size pieces. When ready to serve, combine ingredients in a chilled bowl. Toss with a clear French dressing.

Serves 4

Texas Beef Salad

One 12-ounce **RATH® Breakfast Beef**, cut into small pieces and browned
1 head lettuce, chopped
1 medium onion, minced
4-5 tomatoes, diced
1 can pinto beans, rinsed and drained
1 cup Cheddar cheese, grated
¼ cup catsup
⅛ teaspoon chili powder
¼ teaspoon oregano
Dressing:
½ cup hot or mild taco sauce
½ cup mayonnaise

1 bag taco-flavored tortilla chips, crushed.

Combine first 9 ingredients. Add dressing and mix well. Add crushed tortilla chips just before serving.

Marinated Sausage Salad

1 pound **WILSON® Smoked Sausage**
⅓ cup olive oil
¼ cup red wine vinegar
¼ teaspoon oregano, crushed
¼ teaspoon sugar
2 medium tomatoes, cut in wedges
1 medium green pepper, cut in strips
½ cup ripe olives, halved
#1 head romaine lettuce, torn

Slice sausage in ¼" pieces. Combine oil, vinegar, oregano, and sugar. Combine with vegetables in bowl 2 hours. Just before serving, toss with romaine. *6 servings*

Sizzlean® 'n Vegetable Salad

7 to 8 slices **SWIFT SIZZLEAN®**, cut into ½ inch pieces
10 ounce package frozen mixed vegetables, prepared according to packaged directions
2 cups torn lettuce
½ cup chopped celery
3 green onions, sliced
1½ tablespoons vinegar
2 hard-cooked eggs, sieved

Panfry **SIZZLEAN®** until crisp. Remove with slotted spoon and drain on paper towel. Combine **SIZZLEAN®**, mixed vegetables, lettuce, celery and onion in large bowl. Add vinegar to **SIZZLEAN®** drippings in skillet. Heat just until flavors are blended, about 4 to 5 minutes. Pour over vegetables and toss lightly. Garnish with sieved eggs. *Yield: 5 cups, 4 to 5 servings*

Gallo®-rious Layered Salad

1 cup elbow macaroni
4 cups shredded lettuce
4 carrots, sliced
10 oz. pkg. frozen peas
1 small red onion, sliced
3 oz. **GALLO® Italian Dry Salame**, julienned strips
1½ cups mayonnaise
1½ tsp. dill weed
½ tsp. salt
½ cup shredded Swiss cheese

Cook macaroni as directed on package; drain and chill. In 3 quart clear glass salad bowl, layer lettuce, carrots, macaroni, peas, onion, and salame. Combine mayonnaise, dill weed and salt; mix well. Spread evenly over top of salad. Sprinkle with cheese. Cover and chill several hours or overnight. *6-8 servings*

Oriental Sprout Salad

1 package (8 oz.) **OSCAR MAYER Sliced Peppered Loaf**
5 cups (about 12 oz.) Chinese or celery cabbage, thinly sliced
2 cups homegrown sprouts or 1 can (16 oz.) bean sprouts, drained
1 cup sliced fresh mushrooms
1 can (8 oz.) sliced water chestnuts, drained
1 package (7 oz.) frozen snow peas, thawed
2 green onions with tops, chopped
2 tablespoons sesame seeds

Salad Dressing:
½ cup soy sauce
¼ cup vinegar
2 tablespoons oil
2 teaspoons sugar
6 drops bottled hot pepper sauce
Dash dry mustard

Cut stacked sliced meat into ¼-inch strips; separate strips. Place Chinese cabbage into large salad bowl. In medium bowl combine meat, sprouts, mushrooms, water chestnuts, peas and onions; toss. Place on top of cabbage. In large heavy skillet over medium-high heat, toast sesame seeds 2 to 3 minutes stirring often until golden brown. Sprinkle over meat mixture.

In small bowl combine remaining ingredients; blend well. Pass dressing with salad. *Makes 4 (1½ cup) servings*

Note: For fuller flavor marinate mushrooms 1 hour in salad dressing.

Tropical Ham Salad

3 cups **OSCAR MAYER Ham** cubes (½") OR 2 packages (8 oz. each) **OSCAR MAYER Ham Slices** cut into ½" cubes
1 can (1 lb.) orange and grapefruit sections, chilled
¼ cup flaked coconut
Lettuce leaves
1 avocado, peeled and cut into wedges

Dressing:
½ cup (4 oz.) sour cream
1½ teaspoons sugar
½ teaspoon horseradish
¼ teaspoon salt
Dash dry mustard

Drain orange and grapefruit sections, reserving 1 tablespoon liquid. Gently combine orange and grapefruit sections with ham, avocado wedges and coconut in bowl. Spoon ham and fruit mixture onto lettuce leaves.

DRESSING:
Whip sour cream until fluffy, about 1 minute. Fold in 1 tablespoon orange and grapefruit liquid and remaining ingredients. Serve with salad. *Makes 4 servings*

Southwestern Salad Bowl

½ head lettuce shredded
1 pound ground beef
½ teaspoon salt
1 medium onion, chopped
1 15-ounce can kidney beans, drained
1 cup grated American cheese
2 medium tomatoes, cut in wedges
½ cup ripe olives
2 cups **DORITOS® Brand Taco Flavor Tortilla Chips**
Tomato Sauce*

Sauté beef, salt and onion in skillet. Add drained beans; heat through. In a large salad bowl, layer in order: lettuce, **DORITOS® Brand Taco Flavor Tortilla Chips**, beef and bean mixture, cheese and Tomato Sauce*. Repeat. Garnish with tomato wedges, ripe olives, cheese and whole **DORITOS® Brand Taco Flavor Tortilla Chips**.

Makes 6 servings

*Tomato Sauce

1 8-ounce can tomato sauce
½ medium onion, chopped fine
½ medium tomato, cut into small pieces
¼ teaspoon chili powder

Mix together and simmer for 10 minutes.

General Mills

Betty Crocker® Taco Salad

1 pound ground beef
1 package **BETTY CROCKER® HAMBURGER HELPER® Mix for Cheeseburger Macaroni**
3⅓ cups hot water
2 to 3 teaspoons chili powder
1 large clove garlic, crushed
Dash of cayenne pepper, if desired
6 cups shredded lettuce
1 medium green pepper, chopped (about 1 cup)
2 medium tomatoes, chopped (about 1½ cups)
⅓ cup sliced green onions (with tops)
¼ cup sliced ripe olives

Cook and stir ground beef in 10-inch skillet until brown; drain. Stir in Macaroni, Sauce Mix, water, chili powder, garlic and cayenne pepper. Heat to boiling, stirring constantly; reduce heat. Cover and simmer, stirring occasionally, 15 minutes. Uncover and cook 5 minutes longer.

Place lettuce, green pepper, tomatoes, onions and olives in large bowl; toss with ground beef mixture. Serve immediately or, if desired, cover and refrigerate until chilled, at least 4 hours. Serve with tortilla chips and dairy sour cream if desired.

6 to 8 servings

Wyler's® Taco Salad

1 pound lean ground beef
1 (16-ounce) can stewed tomatoes
1 (4-ounce) can chopped green chilies, drained
2 teaspoons **WYLER'S® Beef-Flavor Instant Bouillon or 2 Beef-Flavor Bouillon Cubes**
¼ teaspoon hot pepper sauce
⅛ teaspoon garlic powder
Dash pepper
1 quart shredded lettuce (1 medium head)
1 to 1½ cups corn chips
1 medium tomato, chopped (about 1 cup)
1 cup (4 ounces) shredded Cheddar cheese

In large skillet, brown meat; pour off fat. Add remaining ingredients except lettuce, corn chips, chopped tomato and cheese. Simmer uncovered 30 minutes. In large bowl or platter, arrange all ingredients; toss to serve. Refrigerate leftovers.

Makes 4 servings

Wolf® Brand Taco Salad

1 - 10 oz. can **WOLF® Brand Chili w/Beans** (heated)
2½ - cups shredded lettuce
½ - cup ripe olive slices
1 - medium-sized tomato, chopped
1 - cup guacamole
½ - cup (2 oz.) shredded Cheddar cheese
2 - cups corn chips

In 2-qt. glass salad bowl, layer hot chili, lettuce, olives, and tomato. Spoon guacamole over tomato; top with cheese and corn chips. Serve immediately.

Serves 2 or 3

Taco Salad

½ lb. ground beef
1 tsp. chili powder
½ tsp. gound cumin
¼ tsp. salt
½ head iceberg lettuce, torn (about 6 cups)
2 cups tortilla chips
1 (16 oz.) can **VEG-ALL® Mixed Vegetables**, drained
1 medium tomato, cubed
½ lb. Monterey Jack cheese, diced
¼ cup green onions, sliced

For dressing, blend together:
½ cup mild taco sauce
½ cup sour cream

In a small skillet brown beef with spices and salt. Crumble meat as it cooks. Cool. Combine lettuce and taco chips in large salad bowl. Next, mound **VEG-ALL®** in center. Surround with beef, tomato, cheese and onions. Add dressing and toss at table just before serving.

Serves 4

Pasta Salads

Seafood Salad With Crab Louis Dressing

3 quarts water
3 teaspoons salt
1 tablespoon oil
2½ cups **AMERICAN BEAUTY® SHEL-RONI®**
6-oz. pkg. frozen cooked crab, thawed and drained
10-oz. pkg. frozen cooked shrimp, thawed and drained
½ cup sliced celery
½ cup quartered ripe olives
½ cup chopped green pepper
¾ cup chili sauce
½ cup mayonnaise
5 tomatoes, cut in sixths
Lettuce leaves

Boil water in large deep pot with salt and oil (to prevent boiling over). Add **SHEL-RONI®**; stir to separate. Cook uncovered after water returns to a full rolling boil for 10 to 11 minutes. Stir occasionally. Drain and rinse under cold water.

In large bowl, combine cooked **SHEL-RONI®**, crab, shrimp, celery, olives and green pepper; cover and refrigerate for at least 1 hour. In small bowl, combine chili sauce and mayonnaise. Cover and refrigerate for at least 1 hour.

Line individual salad bowls with lettuce leaves. Place 1 cup of salad in each bowl. Garnish each salad with 3 tomato wedges and serve with dressing. *10 servings*

HIGH ALTITUDE—Above 3500 Feet: Cooking times may need to be increased slightly for **SHEL-RONI®**; no additional changes.

NUTRITION INFORMATION PER SERVING
SERVING SIZE: ⅒ of recipe

		Percent U.S. RDA
Calories	294	Per Serving
Protein	15g	Protein	23
Carbohydrate	30g	Vitamin A	21
Fat	13g	Vitamin C	41
Sodium	663mg	Thiamine	14
Potassium	359mg	Riboflavin	8
		Niacin	13
		Calcium	7
		Iron	15

San Giorgio®
Garbanzo Pasta Salad

1½ cups **SAN GIORGIO® Ditalini**, uncooked
½ teaspoon salt
1 clove garlic
2 cups (16 ounces) chick peas, drained
¼ cup minced onion
¼ cup minced parsley
¼ cup chopped pimiento
¼ cup olive oil or vegetable oil
2 tablespoons red wine vinegar or lemon juice

Cook Ditalini according to package directions; drain well. Cool. (Rinse with cold water to cool quickly; drain well.)

Crush garlic and salt together in salad bowl. Add cooled Ditalini, chick peas, onion, parsley, pimiento, oil and vinegar. Toss lightly until all ingredients are well blended. Chill.
4 to 6 servings

San Giorgio®
Pasta Primavera Salad

2½ cups (8 ounces) **SAN GIORGIO® Shell Macaroni**, uncooked
2 cups cherry tomatoes, halved
1 cup fresh broccoli flowerettes
1 cup thinly sliced zucchini
1 cup sliced fresh mushrooms
½ cup chopped onion
2 tablespoons minced fresh parsley
½ cup bottled Italian salad dressing

Cook Shell Macaroni according to package directions; drain well. Cool. (Rinse Shell Macaroni with cold water to cool quickly; drain well.) Combine cooled Shell Macaroni with remaining ingredients and toss lightly. Chill. *4 to 6 servings*

Chicken and Spagetti Salad With Raw Vegetables

½ pound Spaghetti, cooked according to package directions and drained
1 bottle (8 ounces) herb and garlic salad dressing
3 cups cooked chicken, diced
¼ cup mayonnaise
1 pint cherry tomatoes, halved
1 cup green onions or scallions, sliced
¼ pound fresh mushrooms, sliced
1 large green pepper, thinly sliced
1½ cups **PEPPERIDGE FARM® Cheese and Garlic Croutons**

Toss hot spaghetti with ¾ cup salad dressing (reserve remainder); cover and chill 2 to 12 hours. *Just before serving:* Toss chicken with mayonnaise and then with marinated pasta. Arrange on platter and top with tomato, onions, mushrooms and pepper. Sprinkle with croutons; toss and serve. *Makes 6 main-dish servings*

Wish-Bone® Pasta Primavera Salad

½ pound rotelle macaroni*
1 cup (8 oz.) **WISH-BONE® Sour Cream & Italian Herbs Dressing**
¼ cup milk
2 tomatoes, coarsely chopped
1 cup sliced mushrooms
½ cup pitted ripe olives
1 green or red pepper, cut into thin strips

Cook macaroni according to package directions; drain and rinse with cold water until completely cool. In large bowl, blend sour cream and Italian herbs dressing with milk; stir in tomatoes, mushrooms, olives and green pepper. Add macaroni and toss well; chill. *Makes about 4 servings*

*Substitution: Use ½ pound ziti or shell macaroni.

Italian Garden Salad

3 quarts water
3 teaspoons salt
1 tablespoon oil
3⅓ cups **AMERICAN BEAUTY® Mostaccioli** or 3 cups **RONI-MAC®**
⅓ cup tarragon vinegar
¼ cup oil
2 teaspoons dill weed
1½ teaspoons salt
½ teaspoon dry mustard
¼ teaspoon pepper
1 garlic clove, minced
2 cups (4 small) chopped tomatoes
2 cups (2 to 3 medium) sliced zucchini
2 cups pitted ripe olives

Boil water in large deep pot with 3 teaspoons salt and 1 tablespoon oil (to prevent boiling over). Add mostaccioli; stir to separate. Cook uncovered after water returns to a full rolling boil for 11 to 12 minutes. Stir occasionally. Drain and rinse under cold water. In small bowl, combine vinegar, ¼ cup oil, dill weed, 1½ teaspoons salt, mustard, pepper and garlic. In large bowl, combine cooked mostaccioli, tomatoes, zucchini and olives. Pour dressing over salad mixture; toss well to combine ingredients. Chill for at least 1 hour to blend flavors. *22 (½-cup) servings*

High Altitude—Above 3500 Feet: Cooking times may need to be increased slightly for mostaccioli; no additional changes.

NUTRITIONAL INFORMATION PER SERVING

SERVING SIZE: 1/22 of recipe		PERCENT U.S. RDA PER SERVING	
Calories	90		
Protein	2 g	Protein	3
Carbohydrate	11 g	Vitamin A	4
Fat	4 g	Vitamin C	10
Sodium	220 mg	Thiamine	5
Potassium	96 mg	Riboflavin	3
		Niacin	3
		Calcium	—
		Iron	3

Chicken of the Sea®

Picnic Tuna-Seashell Salad

⅔ cup dairy sour cream
⅔ cup mayonnaise or salad dressing
¼-½ teaspoon salt
⅛ teaspoon ground white pepper
⅛ teaspoon dill weed
1 can (9¼ oz.) **CHICKEN OF THE SEA® Chunk Light Tuna**, drained and flaked
4 ounces (1 cup raw) small seashell macaroni, cooked and drained
4 ounces (1 cup) diced Muenster cheese
½ cup chopped celery
¼ cup sliced stuffed olives
¼ cup thinly sliced sweet gherkins
¼ cup sliced green onions with tops
¼ cup chopped cucumber
2 tablespoons chopped green pepper

In a large bowl, combine sour cream, mayonnaise, salt, pepper and dill weed. Add remaining ingredients. Toss gently to coat. Chill several hours to blend flavors. If desired, serve on lettuce leaves; garnish with tomato wedges or green pepper rings. *Makes about 5½ cups*

San Giorgio®

Greek Rotini Salad

3 cups **SAN GIORGIO® Rotini**, uncooked
2 tablespoons lemon juice
½ cup olive oil or vegetable oil
½ teaspoon salt
¼ teaspoon pepper
¼ teaspoon dried oregano
1 clove garlic, crushed
2 tomatoes, cut into wedges
1 cucumber, peeled and thinly sliced
1 cup thinly sliced green pepper strips
12 black olives or Greek olives
1½ cups (6 ounces) crumbled Feta cheese
8 red radishes, thinly sliced
¼ cup (about 4) green onions, sliced
2 tablespoons chopped parsley

Cook Rotini according to package directions; drain well. Cool. (Rinse with cold water to cool quickly; drain well.)

Combine lemon juice, oil, salt, pepper, oregano and crushed garlic in screw top jar or small bowl. Shake well or whip with wire whisk until blended and of a thick and creamy consistency. Chill.

Combine cooled Rotini, tomato wedges, cucumbers, green peppers, olives, Feta cheese, radishes, green onions and parsley in large bowl. Pour dressing over salad and toss gently to coat pasta and vegetables evenly. Serve immediately. *6 to 8 servings*

BLUE DIAMOND® the Almond People®

Japanese Noodle Salad

¾ pound spinach
2½ quarts water
1 tablespoon salt
6 ounces egg noodles
1 cup sliced mushrooms
⅔ cup **BLUE DIAMOND® Blanched Slivered Almonds**, toasted*
½ cup sliced green onion
¼ pound cooked ham cut in julienne slices
Dressing (recipe follows)

Wash spinach thoroughly; remove stems. In large kettle, bring water and salt to a boil; add noodles, reduce heat and slowly boil 4 to 5 minutes; add spinach and cook one minute more, or until noodles are tender. Drain thoroughly. In large bowl combine noodles and spinach with mushrooms, almonds, onion and ham. Pour dressing over and lightly toss; chill.

Makes 4 servings

***To Toast Almonds:** Spread in single layer in shallow pan. Bake, stirring often in 300°F. oven 15 minutes, or until they begin to turn color. *Don't wait for them to become golden brown.* After removing the almonds from the oven, their residual heat will continue to toast them slightly.

Dressing

Thoroughly blend ¼ cup vegetable oil, 2 tablespoons soy sauce, 1 tablespoon dry sherry, and ⅛ teaspoon ginger.

Salmon Pasta Salad

8 oz. pkg. small shell macaroni
1¼ cups Italian Dressing & Marinade
2 Tbsp. lemon juice

Cook macaroni according to package directions, drain—combine with dressing and lemon juice and chill 1 hr.

To Serve:
15½ oz. can GILLNETTERSBEST Red Sockeye Salmon*
1½ cups sliced celery
2 medium tomatoes, cubed
2 green onions, chopped
2 hard cooked eggs, chopped
Ripe olives
Parsley

Drain salmon and separate into bite size chunks. In a salad bowl, combine salmon, macaroni, celery, tomato, green onion and egg. Garnish with ripe olives and parsley. Sprinkle additional dressing over salad and toss gently.   *Serves 6-8*

*DEMING'S, DOUBLE Q or HUMPTY DUMPTY Salmon may be substituted.

Ronzoni®
Elbow Macaroni Salad

1 tablespoon salt
3 qts. boiling water
2 cups (8 oz.) RONZONI® Elbow Macaroni
½ cup mayonnaise
2 tablespoons lemon juice
½ teaspoon salt
2 tablespoons chopped pimiento
2 tablespoons chopped chives
2 ripe tomatoes, cut in wedges
4 hard-boiled eggs (chopped)
2 tablespoons chopped olives (optional)

Add 1 tablespoon salt to rapidly boiling water. Gradually add macaroni so that water continues to boil. Cook uncovered, stirring occasionally, until tender. Drain in colander. Rinse with cold water; drain well. Combine mayonnaise, lemon juice and ½ teaspoon salt; blend. Combine macaroni, pimientos, chives and chopped eggs; toss lightly. Combine macaroni mixture and mayonnaise mixture. Toss lightly but thoroughly. Serve on lettuce, garnished with tomato wedges. Sprinkle with chopped olives, if desired.

Mueller's®
Celebration Salad

Cooked asparagus spears
Bottled Italian dressing
8 ounces (2 cups) MUELLER'S® Elbow Macaroni
¾ cup mayonnaise
2 tablespoons ketchup
½ teaspoon prepared horseradish
¼ teaspoon dry mustard
2 tablespoons sliced scallions
2 cups slivered cooked ham
1 cup sliced celery
Watercress
Cherry tomatoes

Marinate asparagus in Italian dressing over night, or at least 3 to 4 hours. Cook macaroni as directed on package; drain. Rinse with cold water; drain again. In bowl blend mayonnaise, ketchup, horseradish, mustard and scallions; toss in macaroni, ham and celery. To serve, arrange asparagus spears on platter; top with macaroni salad. Garnish with watercress and cherry tomatoes.   *6 servings*

Macaroni & Cheese Salad

1 cup mayonnaise
¼ cup milk
2 cups (8 oz.) SARGENTO Shredded Cheddar Cheese
2 cups cooked elbow macaroni
2 large tomatoes, diced
2 cups diced celery
1 small onion, chopped
½ green bell pepper, diced
1 teaspoon salt
¼ teaspoon garlic salt

Blend mayonnaise with milk. Combine remaining ingredients; mix thoroughly with dressing. Chill.   *Makes 4-6 servings*

Macaroni Salad Supreme

4 cups cooked elbow macaroni, drained and rinsed
½ cup each chopped celery and green pepper
¼ cup each finely chopped scallions and parsley
3 Tbsp. wine vinegar
¾ cup mayonnaise
4 Tbsp. (2 oz.) ROMANOFF® Caviar*
Crisp salad greens

Combine macaroni with vegetables. Stir vinegar into mayonnaise along with caviar. Add to macaroni; mix well. Chill. Serve on salad greens.   *Makes 8 servings*

*ROMANOFF Red Salmon Caviar suggested

Macaroni Shell Salad
à la Russe

2 cans (15 oz. each) CHEF BOY-AR-DEE® Macaroni Shells
½ cup mayonnaise
1 medium onion, grated
1 tablespoon chopped fresh dill or ½ teaspoon dried dill weed
½ lb. shrimp, cooked, shelled and chopped, or 1 can (7½ oz.) tuna, flaked
1 cup chopped celery
¼ cup dairy sour cream
1 tablespoon vinegar
2 teaspoons sugar

Pour macaroni shells into medium-size bowl. Add remaining ingredients; chill for at least one hour.

Party Chicken Macaroni Salad

1 (3-pound) broiler-fryer chicken, cooked and meat removed from bones and cubed (about 3 cups)
1 (7-ounce) package *or* 2 cups uncooked **CREAMETTES® Elbow Macaroni**, cooked as package directs, rinsed and drained
1 cup chopped celery
1 tablespoon grated orange rind
2 medium oranges, peeled and sliced
1 cup seedless white grapes
½ to 1 cup mayonnaise or salad dressing
½ to 1 cup sour cream
1 teaspoon salt
3 tablespoons sliced maraschino cherries
Lettuce leaves
½ cup toasted nuts

In large bowl, combine all ingredients except cherries, lettuce and nuts. Mix well. Chill thoroughly. Just before serving, stir in cherries; serve on lettuce garnished with nuts. Refrigerate leftovers.
Makes 8 to 10 servings

Mama Mia Macaroni Salad

2 cups salad macaroni, uncooked (4 cups cooked)
1 can (3 oz.) **BinB® Sliced Mushrooms**, undrained
1 package (10 oz.) frozen Italian green beans, cooked
2 tablespoons vegetable oil
2 tablespoons wine vinegar
½ teaspoon salt
¼ teaspoon each basil, oregano, celery seed
⅛ teaspoon pepper
Sliced pepperoni (4 oz.), cut in small pieces
¼ cup mayonnaise

Cook macaroni according to package directions. Drain. Cook green beans until tender-crisp and drain. Combine mushrooms including buttery broth, oil, vinegar, salt, basil, oregano, celery seed and pepper. Toss lightly with macaroni, pepperoni, and beans. Chill well. Just before serving, toss with mayonnaise.
Serves 4 to 5

Mueller's
Macaroni Smorgasbowl

8 ounces (2 cups) **MUELLER'S® Elbow Macaroni**
½ cup mayonnaise
½ cup sour cream
1 teaspoon salt
1 cup sliced celery
½ cup diced cucumber
½ cup shredded carrot
¼ cup diced green pepper
¼ cup chopped parsley
2 tablespoons sliced scallions
2 tomatoes, diced

Cook macaroni as directed on package; drain. Rinse with cold water; drain again. In bowl blend mayonnaise, sour cream and salt; add macaroni and vegetables; toss. Serve on crisp greens; offer a selection of foods such as flaked tuna, sliced cooked frankfurters, cheese cubes and pickled beets to be added to each helping of salad as desired.
6 servings

Luncheon Salad

(Low Calorie)

1 (7 ounce) package or 2 cups uncooked **CREAMETTES® Elbow Macaroni**, cooked as package directs, rinsed and drained
1 (7 ounce) can tuna packed in water, drained and flaked
4 slices low calorie cheese, cut into small pieces
½ cup chopped green pepper
2 tablespoons chopped pimiento
6 tablespoons bottled low calorie Italian dressing
2 tablespoons lemon juice
1 to 2 tablespoons prepared horseradish
½ teaspoon garlic salt
2 tablespoons chopped parsley
8 medium tomatoes (cut into wedges, cutting to, but not through, bases)

In large bowl, combine all ingredients except tomatoes; mix well. Chill thoroughly. Serve in tomatoes. Refrigerate leftovers.
Makes 8 servings

VARIATION:

Add 2 cups chopped fresh tomatoes to salad mixture, serve on lettuce instead of in tomatoes.

Calories: Prepared as directed, provides approximately 180 calories per serving.

Macaroni Medley

2 cups uncooked elbow macaroni
1 medium cucumber, peeled, chopped
½ cup chopped onion
2 tablespoons chopped parsley
2 tablespoons chopped pimiento
1½ cups **HEINZ Apple Cider Vinegar**
¾ cup granulated sugar
1 tablespoon salad oil
1 teaspoon **HEINZ Mild Mustard**
¾ teaspoon salt
½ teaspoon pepper
½ teaspoon garlic powder

Cook macaroni following package directions. Drain; rinse in cold water; drain again. In large bowl, combine cooked macaroni, cucumber and next 3 ingredients. In large jar, combine vinegar and remaining ingredients; cover; shake well to blend. Pour over macaroni mixture; toss. Cover; refrigerate overnight.
Makes 6-8 servings (about 6½ cups)

NOTE: Macaroni will keep about a week when stored tightly covered in the refrigerator.

Hearty Macaroni Salad

4 cups cooked elbow macaroni
½ cup sliced celery
1 cup shredded Cheddar cheese
1 cup mayonnaise
1 teaspoon McCORMICK®/SCHILLING® Instant Minced Onion
2 teaspoons McCORMICK®/SCHILLING® SEASON-ALL® Seasoned Salt
¼ teaspoon McCORMICK®/SCHILLING® Black Pepper
¼ teaspoon McCORMICK®/SCHILLING® Dry Mustard
¼ cup McCORMICK®/SCHILLING® Imitation Bacon Chips

Combine macaroni, celery and cheese. Mix mayonnaise with onion, **SEASON-ALL®**, pepper and dry mustard. Pour over salad and toss to mix well. Chill. Mix in bacon chips before serving.

Makes 6 servings

salad crispins.

Macaroni-Cheddar Salad

1 cup elbow macaroni, uncooked
1 cup cubed Cheddar cheese
½ cup chopped celery
¼ cup chopped green pepper
2 tablespoons chopped onion
2 tablespoons chopped pimiento
¾ cup mayonnaise
⅓ cup sweet pickle relish
1 tablespoon vinegar
1 teaspoon mustard
½ teaspoon dill weed
¼ teaspoon salt
¾ cup SALAD CRISPINS®, AMERICAN STYLE

Cook macaroni according to package directions; rinse, drain and cool. Combine mayonnaise, pickle relish, vinegar, mustard, dill weed and salt. Toss together macaroni, cheese, celery, green pepper, onion and pimiento. Top with mayonnaise mixture and toss to coat macaroni. Chill several hours. Top with **SALAD CRISPINS®** before serving. *Makes 6 servings*

Fiesta Mac Salad

1 7¼-oz. pkg. **KRAFT Macaroni and Cheese Dinner**
1 cup chopped tomato
½ cup chopped cucumber
½ cup shredded carrot
½ cup **MIRACLE WHIP Salad Dressing**
¼ teaspoon salt

Prepare Dinner as directed on package. Add remaining ingredients; mix lightly. Chill. Add additional salad dressing before serving, if desired. *4 to 6 servings*

Curry Macaroni Salad

1 package (8 oz.) macaroni (2 cups uncooked)
1 tablespoon butter or margarine
1½ teaspoons curry powder
1 cup finely chopped onion
1 cup thinly sliced celery
¼ cup raisins
½ cup dairy sour cream
¼ cup mayonnaise
¼ cup **KIKKOMAN Soy Sauce**
1 tablespoon lemon juice

Prepare macaroni according to package directions for salad use; drain and turn into medium-size bowl. Melt butter in small pan. Stir in curry and onion; cook and stir over high heat 1 minute. Combine onion mixture with macaroni, celery and raisins. Blend together sour cream, mayonnaise, soy sauce and lemon juice; add to macaroni mixture and toss to combine. Cover and chill at least 2 hours to allow flavors to blend. Just before serving, stir thoroughly. *Makes 6 to 8 servings*

Potato Salads

IMPERIAL Pure Cane SUGAR.

Hill Country Potato Salad

6 medium red potatoes, unpeeled
1 teaspoon salt
½ cup diced raw bacon
½ cup diced onion
1½ teaspoons cornstarch or flour
4 teaspoons **IMPERIAL Granulated Sugar**
1 teaspoon salt
¼ teaspoon pepper
¼ cup cider vinegar
½ cup water
¼ cup minced onion
2 tablespoons snipped parsley
1 teaspoon celery seeds
½ cup sliced radishes, optional
Celery leaves

About 1 hour before serving, cook potatoes in their jackets in boiling water with 1 teaspoon salt in covered saucepan until fork tender, about 35 minutes. Peel and dice or partially mash potatoes. In small skillet, fry bacon until crisp. Add diced onion and sauté until tender but not brown. In bowl, mix cornstarch or flour, **IMPERIAL Granulated Sugar**, 1 teaspoon salt and the pepper. Stir in vinegar and water until smooth. Add to bacon; simmer; stirring until thickened. Pour hot dressing over potatoes and add ¼ cup minced onion, parsley, celery seeds and radishes. Serve lightly tossed and garnished with celery leaves.

Serves 4 to 6

Note: Potatoes may be diced or sliced rather than mashed but mashing allows a more even penetration of seasonings.

Butter Buds®

Potato Salad
(Low Calorie/Low Fat)

⅓ cup reduced calorie mayonnaise
1 packet **BUTTER BUDS®**
1 tablespoon lemon juice
½ teaspoon celery seed
¼ teaspoon salt
3 cups (4 medium-size) diced, cooked potatoes
¾ cup (about 3 stalks) celery
½ cup (1 medium-size) chopped sweet red pepper
¼ cup (1 small) chopped onion

Combine mayonnaise, **BUTTER BUDS®**, lemon juice, celery seed, and salt. Add potatoes, celery, red pepper, and onion; mix thoroughly. Refrigerate. *6 servings*

Per Serving (¾ cup): Calories: 105; Fat: 4g

Note: By using **BUTTER BUDS®** instead of butter in this recipe, you have saved 125 calories and 47 mg cholesterol per serving.

Zesty Meat 'n Potato Salad

1 cup (8 oz.) **BREYERS® Plain Yogurt**
¼ cup mayonnaise
½ teaspoon salt
Dash of pepper
½ teaspoon dry mustard
1 teaspoon prepared horseradish
1 tablespoon lemon juice
3 cups sliced, hot cooked potatoes (about 1 pound)
½ cup thinly sliced scallions
1 cup diced celery
¼ cup finely chopped dill pickle
3 diced hard cooked eggs
2 cups cubed cooked roast beef, ham, or pork

1. Combine yogurt, mayonnaise, salt, pepper, mustard, horseradish, and lemon juice. Pour over hot potatoes. Cool.
2. Add scallions, celery, pickle, eggs, and meat. Chill.
Makes 6 cups or 5 to 6 servings

Chunk Ham Potato Salad

2 medium potatoes, cooked and sliced
2 Tbsp. Italian salad dressing
1 Tbsp. snipped parsley
1 can **HORMEL Chunk Ham**, flaked with fork
3 cups salad greens (lettuce, spinach, romaine, endive, etc.) torn into bite-size pieces
3 hard-cooked eggs, quartered
¾ cup Swiss cheese strips
½ cup sliced pitted ripe olives
¼ cup chopped green onion
½ cup Italian salad dressing

In salad bowl, sprinkle potatoes with 2 tablespoons salad dressing and parsley. Marinate, covered, in refrigerator for several hours or overnight. Layer remaining ingredients except Italian dressing. Just before serving, pour ½ cup Italian dressing over salad and toss lightly. *Makes 4 servings*

Libby's
Libby's
Libby's®

Reuben Potato Salad

1 can (12 oz.) **LIBBY'S® Corned Beef**, chilled
4 cups cooked diced potatoes (about 2 lbs.)
1 can (8 oz.) **LIBBY'S® Sauerkraut**, rinsed and drained
¾ cup sliced celery
½ cup shredded Swiss cheese
1 cup mayonnaise
2 tablespoons prepared mustard
1 teaspoon crushed caraway seed
¾ teaspoon salt
¼ teaspoon garlic powder
⅛ teaspoon pepper
Lettuce leaves, optional

Remove corned beef from can in one piece and cut into ½-inch cubes. Combine corned beef, potatoes, sauerkraut, celery and cheese in a large bowl; toss lightly to mix. Combine remaining ingredients except lettuce leaves, in small bowl; mix well. Add to corned beef mixture and mix gently. Chill. Carry to the picnic in wooden or plastic bowl, lined with lettuce leaves and covered with film or foil. Or use a covered basket with a glass liner.
Yields 6 to 8 servings

Best Foods®
HELLMANN'S®
Basic Potato Salad

¾ cup finely chopped onion
¼ cup lemon juice
1 tablespoon salt
½ teaspoon dry mustard
¼ teaspoon pepper
4 pounds potatoes, boiled in jackets, peeled and cubed
1½ cups chopped celery
½ cup chopped green pepper
2 cups **BEST FOODS®/HELLMAN'S® Real Mayonnaise**

Stir together onion, lemon juice, salt, mustard and pepper. Pour over hot potatoes tossing to coat evenly. Cover and refrigerate about 1 hour. Stir in celery, green pepper and **Real Mayonnaise**. Chill. *Makes 10 (1 cup) servings*

VARIATIONS:

Ham and Cheese Potato Salad

Follow directions for Basic Potato Salad adding 2 cups cooked, cubed ham and 1 cup cubed Cheddar cheese.
Makes 13 (1 cup) servings

Hot Potato Salad

Follow directions for Basic Potato Salad adding 2 pounds cooked killbasy, cut in ¼-inch slices. Place in 4-quart casserole. Sprinkle top with ½ cup fine dry breadcrumbs and ½ cup grated Cheddar cheese. Bake in 350°F oven 15 minutes or until heated.

Makes 14 (1 cup) servings

Apple-Cheese Potato Salad

Follow directions for Basic Potato Salad adding 4 cups diced apples, ¼ cup crumbled bleu cheese, 2 tablespoons lemon juice and 1 teaspoon celery seed. *Makes 14 (1 cup) servings*

Confetti Potato Salad

Follow directions for Basic Potato Salad adding 1 cup each chopped zucchini, cucumber, radish and carrot.

Makes 14 (1 cup) servings

Herb Potato Salad

Follow directions for Basic Potato Salad adding ¼ cup chopped parsley, ½ teaspoon dried chervil and ½ teaspoon dried tarragon leaves to marinade. Substitute 1 cup dairy sour cream for 1 cup of the **Real Mayonnaise**. *Makes 10 (1 cup) servings*

Harvest Potato Salad

8 medium red potatoes (2½ pounds)
1 pound frankfurters
2 tablespoons vegetable oil
¾ cup chopped onion
½ cup chopped celery
3 tablespoons flour
1 tablespoon sugar
½ teaspoon salt
1 teaspoon dry mustard
⅛ teaspoon pepper
1 cup chicken broth
⅓ cup white vinegar
¼ cup parsley, minced
¾ cup **SALAD CRISPINS®, ITALIAN STYLE**

Cook potatoes, with skins on, in boiling salted water until tender. Peel and slice the drained potatoes. Cut each slice in half. Brown frankfurters in oil. Remove from skillet. Drain and combine with potatoes. Sauté onion and celery in oil remaining in skillet until soft. Blend in flour, sugar, salt, dry mustard and pepper. Stir until bubbly. Add chicken broth and vinegar. Cook and stir until mixture thickens. Pour over potatoes. Sprinkle with parsley. Toss lightly. Top with **SALAD CRISPINS®**. Serve hot.

Makes 8 Servings

General Mills

Green 'n Gold Salad

1 package **BETTY CROCKER® Julienne Potatoes**
1 package (10 ounces) frozen green peas, rinsed and drained
1 medium stalk celery, sliced (about ½ cup)
1 small onion, chopped (about ¼ cup)
½ cup ½-inch cubes Cheddar cheese
Dash of salt
½ cup mayonnaise or salad dressing
Lettuce leaves

Prepare potatoes as directed on package for Stove-Top Method. Pour into large bowl; cover and refrigerate until chilled. Stir remaining ingredients except mayonnaise and lettuce into potatoes; toss with mayonnaise. Cover and refrigerate at least 2 hours. Serve on lettuce leaves. *6 servings*

Continental Potato Salad*

1½ pounds (4 cups) peeled, cooked and diced potatoes
1 pound (3 cups) diced, raw zucchini squash
½ pound sliced fresh mushrooms
1 tomato, diced
¼ cup sliced scallions
½ cup olive or salad oil
2 tablespoons **LEA & PERRINS Worcestershire Sauce**
4 teaspoons lemon juice
1¼ teaspoons salt
1 small clove garlic, crushed
¼ teaspoon coarse ground black pepper
¼ teaspoon oregano leaves

In a large salad bowl combine potatoes, squash, mushrooms, tomato and scallions; set aside. Combine oil, **LEA & PERRINS**, lemon juice, salt, garlic, black pepper and oregano; mix well. Pour over vegetable mixture; toss well. Chill thoroughly. Just before serving, sprinkle with pignola nuts, if desired.

Yield: 6 to 8 portions

*May be prepared in advance of serving.

Old-Fashioned Potato Salad

3-4 cups frozen **ORE-IDA® Southern Style Hash Browns**
1 quart water
1 tablespoon salt
¼ cup mayonnaise
¼ cup dairy sour cream
1 tablespoon sweet pickle juice
½ tablespoon **HEINZ Mustard**
½ teaspoon salt
⅛ teaspoon pepper
¼ cup chopped celery
3 tablespoons diced **HEINZ Sweet Pickles**
2 tablespoons frozen **ORE-IDA® Chopped Onions**
2 hard-cooked eggs, coarsely chopped

In boiling water, in covered saucepan, cook frozen potatoes with salt until fork tender—about 2 minutes after return of boil. Drain well. In serving bowl, combine mayonnaise, sour cream, pickle juice, mustard, salt and pepper; mix until smooth and well blended. Add celery, pickles, onions, eggs and warm potatoes; lightly toss; adjust seasonings. Cover salad, then refrigerate several hours. At serving time, garnish with tomato or hard-cooked egg wedges, if desired. *Yield: 4-6 servings*

Note: For a large salad use one bag (32 ounces) and double all ingredients. *Yield: 8-12 servings*

Roquefort Potato Salad

8 cups cooked new potatoes, diced
2 cups chopped celery
⅓ cup chopped onion
4 hard-cooked eggs, chopped
2 packages (1¼ oz. each) **ROQUEFORT Cheese**, crumbled
1 tablespoon salt
½ teaspoon pepper
1 cup mayonnaise
Assorted cold cuts
Sliced cucumbers

Place all the ingredients, except cold cuts and sliced cucumbers, in a large bowl. Toss gently until well blended. Pack firmly into a bowl. Allow to chill overnight. Unmold. Garnish with additional sieved hard-cooked egg and sliced cucumbers. Arrange cold cuts around salad. *Serves 8*

Favorite recipe from the **Roquefort Association, Inc.**

Ham & Cheese Salad

1 package **FRENCH'S® Au Gratin Potatoes**
2 cups chopped celery
1½ to 2 cups diced cooked ham
½ cup mayonnaise
½ cup undrained sweet pickle relish
Lettuce

Simmer potato slices from package in about 3 cups water 15 minutes, until tender. Drain and chill. Combine with celery and ham. Stir together mayonnaise, pickle relish, and seasoning mix from package of potatoes; add to potato mixture. Toss lightly and chill. Serve on lettuce. *6 servings*

Insalada Pepperidge

3 cups new potatoes, unpeeled, cooked and sliced
2 small zucchini, sliced (about 1½ cups)
1 cup sliced celery
2 medium tomatoes, cut in wedges
½ cup sliced stuffed olives
½ cup olive oil
3 tablespoons wine vinegar
¼ cup chopped parsley
½ teaspoon salt
¼ teaspoon oregano, crushed
⅛ teaspoon pepper
1 cup **PEPPERIDGE FARM® Onion and Garlic Croutons**
3 tablespoons grated Parmesan cheese
Lettuce leaves

In a bowl, combine vegetables. Combine oil, vinegar, parsley and seasonings and mix well. Pour over vegetables; toss to blend. Cover and refrigerate at least 2 hours. To serve, spoon over lettuce leaves and sprinkle with onion and garlic croutons. Sprinkle with grated Parmesan cheese. *Makes 6 to 8 servings*

Sweet and Sour Potato Salad

8 potatoes
½ cup **LINDSAY® Chopped Ripe Olives**
1 stalk celery, chopped
2 hard-cooked eggs, sliced
1 onion, minced
3 sweet-sour pickles, chopped
1 tablespoon minced parsley
4 slices bacon, chopped
2 eggs, well beaten
1 cup sugar
1 teaspoon prepared mustard
½ teaspoon salt
¼ teaspoon cracked pepper
½ cup vinegar, diluted with ½ cup cold water

Boil potatoes in their jackets. When tender, peel and slice. Add olives, celery, hard-cooked eggs, onion, pickle and parsley. Fry bacon until crisp and brown. Beat eggs, add sugar, spices and diluted vinegar. Mix well. Pour egg mixture into hot bacon fat and cook, stirring constantly until thickened. Pour over potato mixture and mix lightly. Serve hot. *Makes 6 servings*

Souper Summer Salads

1 envelope **LIPTON® Onion Soup Mix**
1 cup (8 oz.) sour cream
Milk
¼ cup vinegar
Salt and pepper to taste
6 cups thinly sliced cooked potatoes or cooked elbow macaroni
Salad makings*

In large bowl, blend **LIPTON® Onion Soup Mix**, sour cream, ½ to ¾ cup milk, depending on consistency desired, vinegar, salt and pepper. Add potatoes and salad makings and toss until completely coated; chill.

*Salad Makings

Add any combination of the following: thinly sliced celery, chopped hard-cooked eggs, green pepper, tomato or pimiento or your own favorite salad makings.

Rice Salads

International Rice Salad

1 bag **SUCCESS® Rice**
1 can (8 oz.) English peas, drained
1 cup cubed or shredded Swiss cheese
⅓ cup mayonnaise
¼ cup minced pimiento
1 or 2 green onions, sliced
1 tablespoon Dijon mustard

Cook bag of rice according to package directions. Drain bag and empty rice into mixing bowl. Add the remaining ingredients and toss lightly. Chill. Serve on lettuce leaves or garnish with hard cooked egg, crumbled bacon, or tomato wedges.

Makes 6 servings (about ½ cup each)

Bran Pilaf Salad With Cold Cuts and Fruit

½ cup uncooked long-grain rice
1 cup **NABISCO 100% Bran Cereal**
½ cup thinly sliced celery
¼ cup sliced scallions
¾ cup oil and vinegar dressing
2 navel oranges, peeled and sliced
1 large yellow grapefruit, peeled and sliced
Boston or Iceberg lettuce
8 ounces liverwurst, cubed
6 ounces sliced salami, cut in strips
3 ounces sliced bologna, cut in strips
¼ cup thinly sliced pitted black olives

At least 2 hours before serving cook rice according to package directions; chill. Just before serving toss rice with **NABISCO 100% Bran Cereal**, celery, scallions and ½ cup salad dressing. Sprinkle remaining ¼ cup salad dressing over orange and grapefruit slices; set aside. Line large oval platter with lettuce leaves. Arrange pilaf in wide strip in center. Toss liverwurst, salami and bologna; arrange in two strips either side of pilaf. Place orange and grapefruit slices alternately in two strips at side of meat. Garnish with black olive slices, arranged on either side of center of pilaf.

Serves 6

"End of a Sunny Day" Salad

3 cups cooked rice
1 bottle (8 oz.) **WISH-BONE® Russian Dressing**
¼ cup finely chopped green onions
1 can (8 oz.) pineapple chunks in natural juice, drained (reserve 1 tablespoon juice)
1 tablespoon soy sauce
¾ tablespoon ground ginger
2 cups cubed cooked chicken*
2 medium green peppers, cut into 1-inch chunks
1 can (8½ oz.) water chestnuts, drained and sliced

In medium bowl, combine rice, ⅓ cup red Russian dressing, green onions, and reserved pineapple juice. Pack into lightly greased 3 or 4-cup ring mold; chill.

In medium bowl, combine remaining ⅔ cup red Russian dressing, soy sauce, and ginger. Add chicken, green pepper, pineapple, and water chestnuts; chill, tossing occasionally, at least 2 hours.

To serve, unmold rice ring and fill center with salad mixture. Serve, if desired, on fresh lettuce or spinach leaves.

Makes about 4 servings

*VARIATIONS:

Use 2 cups leftover cooked turkey, beef, or pork.

Wild Rice Summer Salad

1 6 oz. package (1 cup) **SHOAL LAKE Pure Canadian Wild Rice**
¼ cup brown sugar
½ tsp. salt
¼ tsp. pepper
4 hard boiled eggs, sliced
¼ cup onion chopped
⅓ cup mayonnaise
1½ tsp. mustard
⅔ cup frozen peas

1. Cook the wild rice according to the package directions. Chill.
2. Cook the peas according to package directions. Chill.
3. Combine all ingredients and toss and chill.

Uncle Ben's®

Carrot-Raisin Rice Salad

1 cup coarsely shredded carrots
½ cup sliced celery
¼ cup raisins
2 tablespoons finely chopped onion
1½ cups chilled, cooked **UNCLE BEN'S® CONVERTED® Brand Rice**
½ cup mayonnaise
½ cup sour cream
1½ teaspoons lemon juice

Add carrots, celery, raisins, and onion to chilled rice. Combine mayonnaise, sour cream and lemon juice. Stir into rice mixture. Cover and chill before serving.

Makes 4 servings

Shirley's Wild Rice and Kidney Bean Salad

1½ cups uncooked **CHIEFTAIN Wild Rice**
1 cup mayonnaise
1 can drained kidney beans
½ cup diced celery
1 small chopped green pepper
1¼ teaspoon salt
¾ teaspoon pepper
1 small chopped onion

Cook rice as in basic method.* Combine all ingredients and chill.

10 servings

*Basic Method

1. Wash wild rice thoroughly with warm tap water; rinse and drain in strainer until water runs clear. Can also pre-soak several hours.
2. Place wild rice in medium sauce pan with recommended amount of salted water and bring to boil. Chicken or beef broth can be substituted for the water.
3. Simmer covered for about 45 minutes until tender but not mushy. Cooking time may vary some.
4. Drain and rinse.

Ham Rice Slaw

2 cups cubed **ARMOUR STAR® Ham**
2 cups cooked rice
1 cup chopped celery
1 hard-cooked egg, finely chopped
1 medium tomato, chopped
¼ cup grated carrot
¼ cup chopped green pepper
¼ cup chopped sweet pickle
¾ cup mayonnaise
¼ teaspoon salt

Combine all ingredients; mix lightly. Chill. Preparation time: 20 minutes.   *6 to 8 servings*

Rice Salad Vinaigrette

2 cups cooked, cold rice
1 cup sliced carrots
1 cup raw green beans, cut into 1 inch pieces
1 cup raw snow peas
1 cup sliced mushrooms
½ cup sliced radishes
¼ cup sliced green onions
¾ cup oil
1 egg, slightly beaten
¼ cup wine vinegar
1½ teaspoons Dijon mustard
¼ teaspoon salt
⅛ teaspoon pepper
1 cup **PEPPERIDGE FARM® Herb Seasoned Croutons**

In a bowl, combine rice with vegetables. Combine oil, egg, vinegar, mustard, salt and pepper. Pour over rice mixture: toss to blend. Cover and refrigerate at least 2 hours. To serve, spoon onto serving dishes and sprinkle with seasoned croutons.

Makes 6 to 8 servings

Calico Rice

6 slices bacon
1½ cups sliced fresh mushrooms (about ¼ pound)
1 cup diagonally sliced celery
½ cup sliced green onions
2 cans (10½ ounces *each*) **FRANCO AMERICAN Au Jus** or **Chicken Giblet Gravy**
2½ cups quick-cooking rice, uncooked
½ cup shredded carrot
½ teaspoon poultry seasoning
Carrot curls
Parsley

In skillet, cook bacon until crisp; remove and crumble. Pour off all but 2 tablespoons drippings. Brown mushrooms and cook celery and onions in drippings until tender. Add remaining ingredients except carrot curls and parsley; cover. Bring to boil; reduce heat. Simmer 10 minutes or until done; stir occasionally. Garnish with carrot curls and parsley.   *Makes about 5 cups, 10 servings*

Apricot Rice Salad

1 can (16 oz.) **DEL MONTE Lite Apricot Halves**
1 Tbsp. soy sauce
1 tsp. oil
1 tsp. vinegar
1 clove garlic, minced
½ tsp. oregano
¼ tsp. ground ginger
2 cups cooked rice
½ cup diced cooked ham
¼ cup diced green pepper
¼ cup sliced green onion
Lettuce
Alfalfa sprouts
Parsley sprigs

Drain fruit reserving liquid for other recipe uses. In salad bowl, combine soy sauce, oil, vinegar, garlic, oregano and ginger. Stir in rice, ham, pepper and onion. Serve on lettuce-lined plates. Garnish with 2 to 3 apricot halves, sprouts and parsley sprigs.
4 servings

UncleBen's®

Napa Valley Brown Rice Salad

1 cup **UNCLE BEN'S® Select Brown Rice**
1⅓ cups dry white wine
⅓ cup vegetable oil
⅓ cup lemon juice
2 tablespoons sugar
1 teaspoon salt
1 garlic clove, minced
Dash of pepper
2 medium zucchini, thinly sliced
1½ cups sliced fresh mushrooms
1 small red onion, cut into thin rings
2 medium tomatoes, chopped

Cook rice according to package directions, substituting 1⅓ cups wine for 1⅓ cups of the water, and omitting butter. Transfer to large bowl. Combine oil, lemon juice, sugar, salt, garlic and pepper, mixing well; stir into rice. Stir in zucchini, mushrooms, and onion. Chill at least 4 hours. To serve, stir in tomatoes.

Makes 8 to 10 servings, about 8 cups rice salad

Rice Salad Indienne

3 cups cold cooked long grain rice
1 cup fresh bean sprouts
½ cup thinly sliced green onion
½ cup **BLUE DIAMOND® Blanched Slivered Almonds**, toasted*
Curry Dressing (recipe follows)

Combine rice, bean sprouts, onion and almonds; add Curry Dressing and toss to mix well.   *Makes 4 to 6 servings*

*To Toast Almonds: Spread in single layer in shallow pan. Bake, stirring often in 300°F. oven 15 minutes, or until they begin to turn color. *Don't wait for them to become golden brown.* After removing the almonds from the oven, their residual heat will continue to toast them slightly.

Curry Dressing

Mix together ½ cup mayonnaise, ¼ cup plain yogurt, 2 tablespoons chopped chutney, 1 tablespoon soy sauce, 1 teaspoon curry powder and ¼ teaspoon ground ginger.

Makes about 1 cup

Bean Salads

Kidney Bean Salad

1¾ cups kidney beans (1 lb. can drained)
2 cups drained diced tomatoes
1 diced cucumber
½ cup chopped green pepper
¼ cup chopped green onion
2 cups diced **CHEEZ-OLA®** or **COUNT DOWN®**
⅓ cup safflower or corn oil mayonnaise
Salt and pepper to taste

Combine beans, tomatoes (peeled and seeds removed) cucumber, green pepper, onion, cheese and mayonnaise and season. Chill. Arrange in lettuce lined bowl. Good to serve at barbecues or buffets.
6 servings

Crisco OIL

Deluxe Kidney Bean Salad

1 can (16 ounces) kidney beans, drained and rinsed
1 can or jar (4 or 4½ ounces) sliced mushrooms, drained
¾ cup thinly sliced celery (cut diagonally)
½ cup golden raisins
Tarragon French Dressing*
Flaked or shredded coconut

Combine beans, mushrooms, celery, and raisins in a large bowl, tossing lightly. Pour over Tarragon French Dressing and toss lightly until well mixed. Chill in refrigerator. Sprinkle coconut over salad before serving.
4 to 6 servings

*Tarragon French Dressing

¾ cup **CRISCO® Oil**
¼ cup tarragon vinegar
1 teaspoon sugar
¾ teaspoon salt
¼ teaspoon paprika
¼ teaspoon dry mustard
¼ teaspoon pepper
1 clove garlic, halved
¼ teaspoon Worcestershire sauce
⅛ teaspoon thyme

Combine all ingredients in a screw-top jar. Cover tightly and shake vigorously to blend well. Store covered in refrigerator. Shake well before using.

Lea & Perrins Kidney Bean Salad

1 can (15 oz.) kidney beans, drained
½ cup bottled French dressing
¼ cup minced onion
1½ tablespoons **LEA & PERRINS** Worcestershire Sauce

Combine all ingredients. Toss, cover, and chill.

3 to 4 servings

Three Bean Salad

In large bowl, blend ¼ cup **DOMINO®** Liquid Brown Sugar, ½ cup cider vinegar and 1 tsp. salt. Add 1 can (1 pound) drained cut green beans; 1 can (1 pound) drained red kidney beans; 1 package (10 ounces) frozen baby lima beans, cooked and drained; ½ cup chopped onion and ¼ cup chopped green pepper. Toss to mix well. Chill.

Salami Bean Salad

½ cup **VIENNA®** Pure Beef Salami, diced
⅓ cup cut green beans, cooked
⅓ cup cut wax beans, cooked
⅓ cup canned kidney beans
1 tsp. chopped green pepper
1 tsp. chopped onion
2 Tbsp. vinegar
1 Tbsp. salad oil
½ tsp. sugar

Combine all ingredients and mix well. May be made ahead and stored in refrigerator to marinate overnight. Spoon into insulated container.

Note: Keep chilled in office refrigerator until lunch.

Dorman's® Matterhorn Salad

1 cup canned chick peas
2 slices **DORMAN'S®** Swiss, cut into julienne strips
3 tablespoons finely chopped parsley
2 tablespoons finely chopped red onion
3 tablespoons vegetable oil
1 tablespoon vinegar or lemon juice
½ teaspoon garlic salt

Combine all ingredients except oil, vinegar and garlic salt; gently toss until well mixed. Combine remaining ingredients until well blended. Toss with salad. Chill in refrigerator 1 hour.

Serves 6

Mixed Bean Salad

1 15 oz. can **STAR Garbanzo Beans**, drained
1 15 oz. can **STAR Dark Red Kidney Beans**, drained
1 16 oz. can wax beans, drained
1 16 oz. can cut green beans, drained
1 cup sliced celery
1 small red onion, thinly sliced into rings
1 red or green bell pepper, cut into strips
¾ cup **STAR Italian Kitchen Olive Oil**
¾ cup **STAR Italian Kitchen Red Wine Vinegar**
¼-½ cup granulated sugar, to taste
1 tsp. crushed oregano
¼ tsp. garlic powder
⅛ tsp. ground black pepper
Salt to taste

Combine all ingredients, and gently toss. Marinate in refrigerator overnight for maximum flavor. *Serves 6-8*

Range Bean Salad

1 can (15 oz.) red kidney beans, drained
⅓ cup sweet pickle relish
2 hard-cooked eggs, chopped
⅓ cup celery, chopped
¼ cup green onion, chopped
¼ cup green pepper, chopped
½ tsp. prepared mustard
½ cup prepared **HIDDEN VALLEY ORIGINAL RANCH® Salad Dressing**

Combine all ingredients, mix well and refrigerate 1-2 hours to blend flavors. *Makes 4 to 6 servings*

Delicatessen Salad

1 can (1 pound) cut green beans, drained
1 can (1 pound) cut yellow beans, drained
1 can (1 pound) green lima beans, drained
1 can (15 to 15½ ounces) garbanzos, drained*
½ cup chopped green pepper
½ cup chopped onion
1 can (4 ounces) pimiento, chopped (½ cup)
½ cup salad oil
½ cup **HEINZ Wine** or **Apple Cider Vinegar**
½ cup granulated sugar
1 tablespoon salt
1 teaspoon pepper

Combine first 7 ingredients in large glass bowl. Combine salad oil and remaining ingredients in jar; shake vigorously. Pour dressing over bean mixture; toss well. Cover; marinate overnight in refrigerator, stirring occasionally. Serve as a meat accompaniment, relish or drain well and serve in lettuce cups as a salad. *Makes about 7½ cups*

*1 can (15½ to 17 ounces) kidney beans, drained may be substituted.

Note: One package of each (9 ounces) frozen cut green beans, yellow beans, and (10 ounces) green lima beans may be substituted. Cook the frozen beans according to package directions. *Makes about 7½ cups*

Lima Garlic Salad

1 package (10 ounces) frozen lima beans, cooked and drained
1½ cups cherry tomatoes, cut in half
1 medium purple onion, sliced and separated into rings
1 medium green pepper, cored, seeded and cut into strips
½ cup sliced black olives
½ cup olive oil
2 tablespoons lemon juice
1 large clove garlic, minced
½ teaspoon salt
¼ teaspoon basil, crushed
1 cup **PEPPERIDGE FARM® Cheddar and Romano Croutons**
Lettuce leaves
Chopped parsley

In a large bowl, combine vegetables. Blend oil, lemon juice, garlic, salt and basil. Pour over vegetables; toss to blend. Cover and refrigerate at least 2 hours. To serve, spoon over lettuce leaves and sprinkle with croutons. Garnish with parsley. *Makes 4 to 6 servings*

Polka Dot Bean Salad

1 can (15-oz.) **NALLEY®'S Chili With Beans**
1 can (15-oz.) garbanzo beans
2 sliced green onions and part of tops
2 medium stalks celery, chopped
¼ cup chopped **NALLEY®'S Dill Pickles**
¼ cup chopped pimiento
2 to 3 Tbsp. wine vinegar
½ tsp. salt

Pour Chili into bowl. Drain and rinse garbanzos and add along with remaining ingredients. Mix gently. Marinate several hours or overnight. *Makes 6 servings*

Garlic Bean Salad

½ cup **KARO® Dark Corn Syrup**
½ cup cider vinegar
¼ cup **MAZOLA® Corn Oil**
1 teaspoon salt
¼ teaspoon pepper
1 can (16 oz.) chick peas, drained
1 can (16 oz.) whole cut green beans, drained
1 can (16 oz.) kidney beans, drained
⅔ cup chopped pitted ripe olives
½ cup sliced green onion
1 clove garlic, minced

Mix together corn syrup, vinegar, corn oil, salt and pepper. Pour over remaining ingredients, stirring until coated. Cover; chill 3 hours or overnight. Drain before serving. *Makes about 6 cups*

Bean Salad

(Insalata de Fagioli)

¼ cup **PROGRESSO Olive Oil**
2 tablespoons **PROGRESSO Wine Vinegar**
2 tablespoons finely chopped onion
½ teaspoon salt
½ teaspoon sugar
¼ teaspoon powdered mustard
⅛ teaspoon ground black pepper
1 can (20 oz.) cannellini (white kidney) beans
1 can (20 oz.) chick peas (ceci)
1 quart torn mixed salad greens
¼ cup roasted peppers, cut in slivers

In a small measuring cup combine oil, vinegar, onion, salt, sugar, mustard and black pepper; mix well and set aside. Drain beans and chick peas thoroughly. Place in separate bowls; pour half of the oil mixture over each bowl of beans; mix well. Cover and refrigerate for at least 1 hour. To serve, place salad greens in a bowl. Arrange beans in alternate clusters on the greens; garnish with roasted peppers. Toss just before serving, sprinkling lightly with oil, vinegar and grated Parmesan cheese, if desired.

Yield: About 6 to 8 portions

Chick Pea Salad Bowl

1 can (20 oz.) chick peas, drained
¼ teaspoon salt
¾ cup thinly sliced celery
1 small onion, thinly sliced
¼ cup chopped green pepper
¼ cup chopped dill pickle
½ cup prepared **GOOD SEASONS® Italian or Mild Italian Salad Dressing**
Dash of pepper

Sprinkle chick peas with salt; let stand about 5 minutes. Add remaining ingredients; mix well. Marinate in refrigerator at least 3 hours. Serve on salad greens, if desired.

Makes 3½ cups or 4 servings

Dorman's® Swiss Almond Salad

2 slices **DORMAN'S® Swiss**, cut into julienne strips
1 cup cooked green beans
3 tablespoons finely chopped onion
½ cup finely chopped almonds
3 tablespoons vegetable oil
1 tablespoon vinegar or lemon juice
Salt
Pepper

Combine all ingredients except oil and vinegar; gently toss until well mixed. Combine remaining ingredients until well blended. Chill in refrigerator 1 hour.

Serves 6

Tangy Bean Salad

½ cup white vinegar
½ cup sugar
½ cup vegetable oil
½ cup chopped onion
½ cup chopped green pepper
1 can (16 ounces) **STOKELY'S FINEST® Cut Green Beans**, drained
1 can (15½ ounces) **STOKELY'S FINEST® Cut Wax Beans**, drained
1 can (15 ounces) **STOKELY'S FINEST® Dark Red Kidney Beans**, drained
Red onion rings (optional)

Combine vinegar, sugar, oil, onion, and green pepper in large bowl and mix well. Drain all beans and add to dressing. Toss gently and marinate in refrigerator for at least 4 hours or overnight. Serve in bowl lined with lettuce. May be garnished with onion rings.

10 servings

Italian Salad

1 medium can tiny whole green beans or French-cut cooked fresh beans
8-10 cherry tomatoes, halved
4 fresh green onions, sliced
½ cup French Dressing II*
BROWNBERRY® Seasoned Croutons

Drain the chilled green beans and gently mix together all ingredients except croutons. Chill at least one hour, or longer if more convenient. Toss in the croutons at serving time, and serve in an ice-cold lettuce lined bowl.

*French Dressing II

¼ cup olive oil
¼ cup peanut oil
¼ cup wine vinegar
1 tsp. paprika
1 tsp. salt
Garlic clove

Combine ingredients in glass jar and shake well. This is enough for a large tossed salad, but any remaining may be stored in refrigerator.

Grecian Green Beans

2 cans (16 oz. each) small whole green beans
2 shallots or small onions
2 cloves garlic
¼ cup cut-up parsley
2 tablespoons sugar
2 teaspoons oregano leaves
2 teaspoons prepared mustard
½ teaspoon salt
½ cup **COCA-COLA®**
¼ cup olive oil
2 tablespoons vinegar

Drain beans and discard liquid. Peel and thinly slice shallots; separate into rings. In large bowl, combine minced garlic with remaining ingredients, stirring until sugar is dissolved. Add beans and shallots; toss lightly with a fork. Pack into a 1-quart glass jar. Cover and refrigerate several hours or overnight for flavors to blend. Serve chilled or as a hot vegetable with steak, hamburger or meat loaf.

Makes 1 quart

Vegetable Salads

CRISCO® OIL

Sweet and Tart Salad

3 cups shredded cabbage
1½ cups chopped apple
½ cup Celery Seed Dressing*

Toss together cabbage and apple. Pour on dressing and toss lightly to coat evenly.   *6 servings*

*Celery Seed Dressing

½ cup sugar
1 teaspoon dry mustard
1 teaspoon salt
4½ tablespoons cider vinegar
1 teaspoon grated onion
1 cup CRISCO® Oil
1 tablespoon celery seed

Mix sugar, mustard, and salt. Blend in 2 tablespoons of the cider vinegar and the grated onion. Gradually beat in CRISCO® Oil. Beat until thick and light. Slowly beat in the remaining cider vinegar. Stir in celery seed. Pour into a screw-top jar. Cover tightly and shake vigorously to blend well. Store covered in refrigerator. Shake well before using.   *About 1⅔ cups*

Tangy Tangerine Coleslaw

Dressing:
¼ cup salad oil
Grated peel of ½ SUNKIST® Tangerine
Juice of 1 SUNKIST® Tangerine (¼ cup)
Juice of ½ SUNKIST® Lemon
2 Tbsp. honey
1 Tbsp. toasted sesame seed (optional)

1 small head cabbage, cut in long thin shreds (about 5 cups)
2 to 3 SUNKIST® Tangerines, peeled, segmented, cut in half, seeded
½ cup raisins
¼ cup chopped nuts

DRESSING:
In jar with lid, combine oil, tangerine peel and juice, lemon juice, honey and sesame seed; shake well.

In large bowl, combine cabbage, tangerines, raisins and salad dressing; chill. To serve, add chopped nuts; toss gently.
    Makes 6 servings (about 7 cups)

Hot Cabbage Slaw

¼ cup BOGGS® Cranberry Liqueur
2 tablespoons REGINA® Red Wine Vinegar
1 egg yolk
1 tablespoon butter (or margarine)
½ teaspoon salt
1 teaspoon sugar
4 cups finely shredded red cabbage
3 slices bacon, crisply cooked and crumbled

In small saucepan, combine BOGGS®, vinegar, egg yolk, butter, salt and sugar. Cook, over medium heat, stirring constantly, until mixture comes to boil. Pour over cabbage. Sprinkle with bacon. Toss. Serve immediately.   *Serves 4-6*

Jif®

Country Cole Slaw

3 cups shredded cabbage
2 tablespoons shredded carrot
2 tablespoons diced onion
2 tablespoons diced green pepper
½ cup dairy sour cream
2 tablespoons JIF® Peanut Butter
2 teaspoons sugar
1 teaspoon salt
2 teaspoons tarragon vinegar

In a large bowl, combine cabbage, carrot, onion, and green pepper. Mix sour cream, JIF®, sugar, salt, and vinegar. Pour over vegetables and toss well. Top with more shredded carrot, if desired.   *Serves 8*

Crisp Overnight Slaw

1½ teaspoons PILLSBURY SWEET* 10® or ¼ cup PILLSBURY SPRINKLE SWEET®
½ teaspoon celery salt
½ teaspoon garlic salt
2 tablespoons lemon juice
2 tablespoons vinegar
3 cups (½ medium head) shredded cabbage
¼ cup chopped green pepper
1 stalk celery, chopped
3 to 4 green onions, sliced
5 to 6 radishes, sliced

In large bowl, combine sweetener, celery salt, garlic salt, lemon juice and vinegar. Add remaining ingredients except radishes; toss lightly. Cover and chill at least 4 hours. Before serving, add radishes.   *6 servings*

Tip: If desired, chopped cucumber, zucchini or halved cherry tomatoes may be added with cabbage.

NUTRITION INFORMATION PER SERVING			
SERVING SIZE: ⅙ of recipe		PERCENT U.S. RDA	
Calories	20	PER SERVING	
Protein	1 g	Protein	*
Carbohydrate	4 g	Vitamin A	*
Fat	1 g	Vitamin C	50%
Sodium	295 mg	Thiamine	2%
Potassium	160 mg	Riboflavin	*
		Niacin	*
		Calcium	2%
		Iron	*

*Contains less than 2% of the U.S. RDA of this nutrient.

Tossed Fish Salad
Lea & Perrins *(Lea & Perrins, Inc.)*

Betty Crocker® Taco Salad
Hamburger Helper® *(General Mills, Inc.)*

Cool Corn Salad *(top)*, Tangy Bean Salad *(center)*, Fiesta Chicken Salad *(bottom)*
Stokely's Finest® *(Stokely-Van Camp, Inc.)*

33

Salad Niçoise
Bac∗Os *(General Mills, Inc.)*

Summer Chef Salad
Durkee *(Durkee Foods-Div. of SCM Corp.)*

Fruited Chicken Salad
American Beauty® *(The Pillsbury Co.)*

Macaroni Shell Salad à la Russe
Chef Boy-Ar-Dee® *(American Home Foods)*

Chicken Salad à la Tarragon
Diet Shasta® *(Shasta Beverages, Sub. of Consolidated Foods)*

Finnish Tuna Salad
Finlandia Swiss Cheese *(Atalanta Corp.)*

Ham Stuffed Avocados *(left)*,
Ham and Pea Stuffed Tomatoes *(right)*
Wilson® *(Wilson Foods Corp.)*

Celebration Salad
Mueller's® *(C.F. Mueller Co.)*

Tropical Ham Salad
Oscar Mayer *(Oscar Mayer Foods Corp.)*

Vegetable Pepperoni Salad
Stokely's®/Stokely's Finest® *(Stokely-Van Camp, Inc.)*

Chicken of the Sea® Mediterranean Tuna Salad
(Ralston Purina Company)

Crisp Liteline Salad
Del Monte *(Del Monte Corp.)*

Fisherman's Favorite Cioppino Salad
Wish-Bone® *(Thomas J. Lipton, Inc.)*

Savory Shrimp Salad *(top)*, Lemon Ginger Chicken Salad *(bottom)*
Best Foods®/**Hellmann's**® *(Best Foods, A Unit of CPC North America)*

Popeye Salad With **Farm-Raised Catfish**
(Catfish Farmers of America)

Chicken and Spaghetti Salad With Raw Vegetables
Pepperidge Farm® *(Pepperidge Farm, Inc.)*

37

Wheat Germ Stuffed Tomato Salad
Kretschmer *(International Multifoods)*

Cream Cheese and Avocado Salad
Calavo® *(Calavo Growers of California)*

Dilled Beefeater's Salad
(Pickle Packers International)

38

Chicken Salad Ambrosia
Swanson *(Campbell Soup Co.)*

''End of a Sunny Day'' Salad
Wish-Bone® *(Thomas J. Lipton, Inc.)*

Oriental Sprout Salad
Oscar Mayer *(Oscar Mayer Foods Corp.)*

Taco Salad *(left)*, Chicken Chow Mein Salad *(center)*,
Tomato Baskets *(right)*
Veg-All® *(The Larsen Company)*

Fiesta Salad Bowl *(top)*, Cheese-Capped Iceberg *(bottom)*
Best Foods®/Hellmann's®
(Best Foods, A Unit of CPC North America)

Sauerkraut Salad
Claussen *(Oscar Mayer Foods Corp.)*

Wolf® Brand Taco Salad
(Wolf Brand Products)

Avocado-Orange Toss
Bac∗Os *(General Mills, Inc.)*

Grecian Green Beans
Coca-Cola® *(The Coca-Cola Company)*

Dorman's® Matterhorn Salad
(N. Dorman & Company)

Italian Salad
Brownberry® *(Brownberry Div. of Oroweat Foods Company)*

Roquefort Salad
Brownberry® *(Brownberry Div. of Oroweat Foods Company)*

Insalada Pepperidge *(top)*, Lima Garlic Salad *(bottom)*
Pepperidge Farm® *(Pepperidge Farm, Inc.)*

(clockwise from top) Garbanzo Pasta Salad, Greek Rotini Salad, Zucchini-Stuffed Tomatoes
P & R/San Giorgio® *(San Giorgio-Skinner Company)*

Old-Fashioned Potato Salad
Ore-Ida® *(Ore-Ida Foods, Inc.)*

Calico Rice
Franco-American *(Campbell Soup Co.)*

Dorman's® Swiss Almond Salad
(N. Dorman & Company)

Napa Valley Brown Rice Salad
Uncle Ben's® *(Uncle Ben's Foods)*

Muffin Pan Fruit Salad *(left)*, Muffin Pan Salad *(right)*
Jell-O® *(General Foods Corp.)*

Tropicana Salad
Hiram Walker (*Hiram Walker Inc.*)

Fruit in the Sun at Midnight
Valio (*Atalanta Corp.*)

Brandied Fruit Salad (*top*), Brandied Chicken-Vegetable Salad (*bottom*)
(*California Brandy Advisory Board*)

Fruit Bowl Salad
Lea & Perrins *(Lea & Perrins, Inc.)*

Royal Pear Salad
Stokely's Finest® *(Stokely-Van Camp, Inc.)*

Vegetable Seafood Aspic
S&W® *(S&W Fine Foods, Inc.)*

Sun World® Summer Salad
(Sun World, Inc.)

46

Chiquita® Banana Orange Melody Salad
(Chiquita Brands, Inc.)

Cranberry Orchard Salad
Jell-O® *(General Foods Corp.)*

California Fruit Salad Rosé
Knox® *(Thomas J. Lipton, Inc.)*

Roquefort Cream Dressing
(Roquefort Association, Inc.)

Nature's Salad Dressing *(left)*, Creamy Salad Dressing *(right)*
Kikkoman *(Kikkoman International)*

Cucumber Parsley Dressing
Dannon® *(The Dannon Company)*

Half Moon Bay Slaw

1 can (8¼ oz.) **DOLE® Crushed Pineapple in Syrup**
1 quart **BUD OF CALIFORNIA® Shredded Cabbage**
1 medium red apple, cored and chunked
1 cup shredded carrots
1 cup sliced celery
½ cup chopped green onions
½ cup salted peanuts
Tangy Blender Mayonnaise*

Drain pineapple well, reserving ¼ cup syrup. Combine pineapple, reserved syrup, cabbage, apple, carrots, celery, onion and peanuts. Toss with Tangy Blender Mayonnaise. Cover; refrigerate at least 1 hour. *Makes 6 servings*

*Tangy Blender Mayonnaise

1 egg yolk
2 teaspoons lemon juice
1 teaspoon Dijon mustard
½ teaspoon salt
½ teaspoon Worcestershire sauce
Dash cayenne pepper
½ cup vegetable oil

Combine egg yolk, lemon juice, mustard, salt, Worcestershire and cayenne in blender. With blender turned on, add oil a few drops at a time. Oil may be added in a continuous drizzle until mayonnaise has thickened. It is best to add oil a few drops at a time at the beginning and end of procedure. *Makes about ¾ cup*

Creamy Hot Slaw

½ cup butter or margarine
1 medium head cabbage, shredded
2 medium onions, chopped
1 cup (8 oz.) **WISH-BONE® Sour Cream & Bacon Dressing**
1 teaspoon caraway seeds

In large saucepan, melt butter and cook cabbage and onions until tender. Remove from heat; stir in remaining ingredients. *Makes about 6 servings*

100% PURE
Minute Maid
FROZEN CONCENTRATED
ORANGE JUICE

Quick Coleslaw

4 cups (½ medium head) shredded cabbage
½ medium cucumber, chopped
¼ cup chopped onion
½ teaspoon celery seed
½ teaspoon salt
1 cup mayonnaise or salad dressing
¼ cup frozen **MINUTE MAID® Orange Juice Concentrate**, thawed and undiluted

In large mixing bowl, combine cabbage, cucumber, onion, celery seed and salt; toss lightly. Combine mayonnaise and orange juice concentrate; pour over cabbage mixture. Toss lightly. Serve immediately. *Makes 4 to 6 servings*

Tropical Cole Slaw

(Low Calorie)

1 head cabbage, finely shredded
1 cup (½ pint) sour cream
1 cup crushed, fresh pineapple or canned in natural juice
1 tablespoon cider vinegar
1 tablespoon **SWEETLITE™ Liquid Fructose**

1. Put the shredded cabbage in a colander and run cold water over it to wash it. Dry thoroughly.
2. Combine all other ingredients in a large bowl and mix thoroughly.
3. Add the washed, thoroughly dried cabbage to the mixture in the bowl and mix it thoroughly again. *Makes 8 servings*

Each serving contains approximately:
½ fruit exchange
1 fat exchange
65 calories
32 mg cholesterol

Sour Cream Cole Slaw

1 cup **MEADOW GOLD® Sour Cream**
2 tablespoons sliced green onion
2 tablespoons vinegar
1½ teaspoons salt
¼ teaspoon ground mustard
⅛ teaspoon pepper
1 small head cabbage, shredded (about 7 cups)

Combine first six ingredients, mixing well. In large bowl, gently toss cabbage and sour cream mixture. Cover. Chill 1 to 2 hours. *6 to 8 servings*

Salad Antipasto

Variety of salad greens torn into bite-sized pieces
Tomatoes cut into sixths—one tomato per serving
Black pitted olives
Red onion cut into rings
Cauliflower separated into flowerets
Zucchini thinly sliced
Italian salad dressing
5 HORMEL Pepperoni sandwich-size slices per person
Swiss cheese, if desired

Combine all ingredients in bowl except dressing and pepperoni. Toss with dressing to coat. Serve on individual salad plates or in bowls. Add 5 rolled-pepperoni slices to each dish. Serve with wedge of cheese if desired.

Dilled Beefeater's Salad

1 quart torn lettuce leaves
¾ pound roast beef strips (about 2 cups)
3 small boiled potatoes, sliced
¼ pound mushrooms, thinly sliced
½ cup sliced celery
6 red or green pepper rings
Beefeater Dressing*
6 dill pickle fans**

Put lettuce in large shallow salad bowl. Arrange roast beef, potatoes, mushrooms, celery and pepper rings on top of greens. Before serving, toss with Beefeater Dressing. Serve in individual salad bowls and add a dill pickle fan. *Makes 6 servings*

*Beefeater Dressing

Combine and mix well ⅔ cup salad oil, ½ cup sliced dill pickles, ¼ cup dill pickle liquid, 1 tablespoon lemon juice, 1¼ teaspoons salt, 1 teaspoon dry mustard, 1 teaspoon Worcestershire sauce, ½ teaspoon thyme and a few grains pepper.

Dill Pickle Fans: Cut dill pickles into 4 lengthwise slices without cutting through pickle end. Spread out sections to form "open fan."

Favorite recipe from **Pickle Packers International**

Greek Salad

1 head lettuce
2 medium tomatoes
1 onion, sliced
1 chopped green pepper
1 cucumber, sliced
½ cup **POMPEIAN Olive Oil**
¼ cup vinegar
Fillets of anchovies or herring

Section lettuce. Add quartered tomatoes, onion, pepper, cucumber. Salt, pepper to taste; mix well. Add **POMPEIAN Olive Oil** and vinegar; toss lightly. Garnish with anchovies or herring bits.
Serves 6

Caviar Vegetable Bowl

2 cucumbers, peeled
2 tomatoes, peeled
2 carrots, pared
¼ cup grated sweet onion and juice
1 pkg. (3 oz.) cream cheese, softened
1 cup sour cream
¼ cup mayonnaise
1 Tbsp. lemon juice
4 Tbsp. (2 oz.) **ROMANOFF® Caviar***
Lettuce leaves

Cut cucumbers in half lengthwise, scoop out seeds. Cut in one-fourth inch thick slices. Halve tomatoes, discard seeds and juice and cut meat into three-fourths inch pieces. Cut carrots into julienne strips. (Food processor may be used.) Stir onion into cream cheese. Blend in sour cream, mayonnaise and lemon juice.
(Continued)

Fold in three tablespoons of the caviar and combine with vegetables. Chill. Serve in lettuce-lined bowl garnished with remaining caviar. *Makes 6 servings*
***ROMANOFF® Black Lumpfish** or **Whitefish** suggested.

Wheat Germ Veggie Salad

1 can (7-8¾ oz.) whole kernel corn, drained
⅓ cup **KRETSCHMER Regular Wheat Germ**
⅓ cup finely sliced green onion
⅓ cup minced parsley
⅓ cup chopped carrots
⅓ cup chopped celery
3 Tbsp. cooking oil
2 Tbsp. lemon juice
½ tsp. basil leaves, crushed
¼ tsp. oregano leaves, crushed
¼ tsp. salt
Salad greens
Sliced cucumber

Combine all ingredients *except* salad greens and cucumber. Mix well. Line salad bowl with greens. Spoon corn mixture into center of greens. Garnish with cucumber. *Makes 4 servings*

Summer Chef Salad

6 cups bite-size pieces mixed salad greens
1½ cups (approx. 6 oz.) turkey ham or ham cut in julienne strips
1 can (11 oz.) **DURKEE Granadaisa Mandarin Orange Segments**, drained
1 cup green seedless grapes
1 can (3 oz.) **DURKEE French Fried Onions**

In a large salad bowl, combine all ingredients except ½ can French fried onions. Drizzle with Wine Vinaigrette Dressing* and toss gently. Serve immediately, garnished with remaining onions.
Makes 6 servings

*Wine Vinaigrette Dressing

¾ cup salad oil
½ cup red wine vinegar
2 teaspoons sugar
½ teaspoon salt
½ teaspoon **DURKEE Tarragon**
¼ teaspoon **DURKEE RedHot! Sauce**

Thoroughly combine all ingredients.

Green Salad

1 bunch of salad greens
1 Tbsp. of Tarragon vinegar
3 Tbsp. **FILIPPO BERIO Olive Oil**
1 clove garlic
⅛ tsp. pepper
⅓ tsp. salt

Thoroughly wash and dry greens. Chill in ice box awhile by wrapping greens in a cloth towel. Rub salad bowl with garlic or use garlic press to put in the garlic juice.
(Continued)

Cut chilled greens into desired pieces, salt slightly. Put salt, pepper, **FILIPPO BERIO Olive Oil** and vinegar in small bowl, mix thoroughly. When dressing is well mixed, pour it into bowl with greens and mix well till all leaves are covered with dressing. Serve at once.

VARIATIONS:

There are many variations of salads, using the same proportions. A dash of **LEA & PERRINS Sauce** may be added to the dressing.

If salad is preferred spicy, add ¼ tsp. dry English mustard to dressing and mix thoroughly.

If lemon juice is preferred, it may be substituted in equal amount for the vinegar.

Black pepper and oregano may be sprinkled on the salad before serving it to give an additional intriguing flavor.

The same dressing may be used on sliced avocados, or slices of avocados may be added to the salad greens.

Avoid putting sliced tomatoes in salad greens. It dilutes the dressing. Make a little more dressing, slice the tomatoes, add salt and pepper. Pour on some of the dressing. Serve separately.

Best Foods® HELLMANN'S®

Fiesta Salad Bowl

½ cup **BEST FOODS®/HELLMANN'S® Real Mayonnaise**
½ cup dairy sour cream
½ cup chopped green onions
½ cup chopped parsley
1 tablespoon lemon juice
1 tablespoon chopped fresh or 1 teaspoon dried dill weed
1 teaspoon salt
1 teaspoon sugar
2 medium zucchini, thinly sliced
1 can (16 oz.) red kidney beans, well drained
¼ pound mushrooms, thinly sliced
2 cups shredded lettuce

Stir together first 8 ingredients; set aside. In 2-quart clear glass bowl place zucchini in one layer; top with ¼ of the **Real Mayonnaise** mixture. Repeat layering with remaining vegetables and dressing. Cover; chill at least 4 hours. Garnish with radish slices and fresh dill. Toss just before serving.   *Makes 8 servings*

Mexican Chef Salad
(Topopo)

4 **VAN DE KAMP'S® Corn Tortillas**—thawed
1 cup refried beans
3 cups shredded lettuce
8 large cooked shrimp; deveined and sliced lengthwise or 1½ cups of other cooked seafood
1 avocado, pitted, peeled and sliced lengthwise (optional)
½ cup finely chopped onion
½ cup shredded Cheddar cheese
½ cup shredded Monterey Jack cheese
1 tomato, cut into wedges or large pieces

Fry tortillas until crisp. Drain well. Spread ¼ cup refried beans on each tortilla. Mound lettuce on tortilla, creating a mountain shape. Arrange shrimp and sliced avocado around the sides of the salad.
(Continued)

Sprinkle with onion, cheese and tomato. If desired, top with bottled taco sauce or hot sauce. Serve at once.
Makes 4 servings

Walnut Tossed Salad

¾ cup large pieces **DIAMOND® Walnuts**
2 tablespoons butter
¼ teaspoon minced or crushed garlic
Orange Vinaigrette Dressing*
1 large or 2 small heads chilled butter lettuce
½ cup thinly sliced red onion rings
1 can (11 ounces) mandarin orange sections, drained

Sauté walnuts in small skillet with butter and garlic over moderately low heat about 5 minutes, until very lightly browned, stirring constantly. Cool. Prepare Orange Vinaigrette Dressing. At serving time, tear lettuce into bite-size pieces to measure 1½ quarts; turn into chilled salad bowl. Top with onion rings, drained orange sections and garlic toasted walnuts. Pour dressing over salad and toss lightly.   *Makes 6 servings*

*Orange Vinaigrette Dressing

Combine ½ cup oil, 3 tablespoons red wine vinegar, ¾ teaspoon salt and 1 teaspoon *each* grated orange peel and basil, crumbled, in a small jar. Cover and shake well to blend. Shake again just before using.   *Makes ¾ cup dressing*

TABASCO®
Cobb Salad With Peppy French Dressing

1 medium head lettuce, coarsely broken
2 cups coarsely chopped watercress leaves
3 hard-cooked eggs, quartered
½ pound bacon, cooked and crumbled
2 medium avocados, peeled, pitted and sliced
2½ cups cut-up cooked chicken
1 tablespoon chopped chives
Lettuce

Combine all ingredients in bowl except lettuce; mix lightly. Line large or individual salad bowls with crisp lettuce. Add salad mixture. If desired, garnish with tomato wedges. Serve with Peppy French Dressing*, and, if desired, additional **TABASCO®**.
Yield: 4 quarts, about 6 to 8 servings

*Peppy French Dressing

⅔ cup salad oil
⅓ cup vinegar
¼ cup catchup
½ teaspoon dry mustard
½ teaspoon paprika
½ teaspoon **TABASCO® Pepper Sauce**
⅛ teaspoon salt
½ teaspoon sugar
2 tablespoons crumbled blue cheese

Combine all ingredients in jar with tight cover. Shake to mix well.
Yield: 1¼ cups

Centennial Iceberg Bowl

1 head **ICEBERG Lettuce**
Gold-Rush Dressing*
1½ cups small cherry tomatoes, whole or halved
1 cup sliced zucchini
1 small red onion, sliced
1 large avocado, sliced

Core, rinse and thoroughly drain lettuce; chill in disposable plastic bag or lettuce crisper. Prepare Gold-Rush Dressing*. When ready to serve, cut lettuce into chunks to measure 1½ quarts. Layer in chilled salad bowl with vegetables. Toss with dressing.
Makes 6 servings

*Gold-Rush Dressing

Measure ½ cup olive oil, ⅓ cup wine vinegar, 2 tablespoons shredded Parmesan cheese, 2 teaspoons onion salt, 1 teaspoon *each* minced garlic, dry mustard and paprika, ½ teaspoon *each* oregano and basil, ⅛ teaspoon pepper and 1 bay leaf into a small jar. Cover tightly and shake well. Shake again before using. If creamier dressing is desired, add 1 beaten egg.
Makes about 1 cup dressing

Favorite recipe from the **California Iceberg Lettuce Commission**

Skinny Chef Salad
(Low Calorie)

2 cups torn salad greens
¼ green pepper, sliced
1 Tbsp. chopped onion
2 slices (2 oz.) **KAHN'S® Cooked Ham**, julienned
1 oz. Swiss cheese, julienned
1 hard cooked egg, quartered
1 cherry tomato
Low calorie commercial salad dressing

In salad bowl combine salad greens, green pepper and onion. Add ham and cheese. Garnish with quartered egg and cherry tomato. Serve with low calorie salad dressing.　*Makes 1 serving*

Note: Low calorie dressings vary in calorie count from 2-30 calories per Tbsp. Check the label.

Calories: 281 calories per serving, plus dressing

TABASCO®
Dad's Favorite Salad

1 large head romaine lettuce
1 can (15¼ ounces) red kidney beans, drained
1 large cucumber, pared and cubed
1 small carrot, pared and shredded
1 bottle (8 ounces) chunky blue cheese dressing
2 tablespoons dry sherry
¼ teaspoon **TABASCO® Pepper Sauce**

Wash romaine, dry, and tear into bite-size pieces, removing coarse ribs. In a large bowl combine romaine, kidney beans, cucumber, and carrot. Mix blue cheese dressing, sherry and **TABASCO®** in small bowl; serve with salad.　*Yield: 6 to 8 servings*

Vegetable Pepperoni Salad

1 package (16 ounces) **Frozen STOKELY'S® Vegetables Milano®**
1 medium-size head lettuce, torn
2 tomatoes, cut in wedges (optional)
4 ounces mozzarella cheese, cubed
2 hard-cooked eggs, diced
½ cup thinly sliced pepperoni
¼ cup sliced scallion (green onion)
2 Tablespoons sliced black olives
½ cup Italian dressing
Salt and pepper to taste
1 jar (4 ounces) **STOKELY'S FINEST® Sliced Pimientos**, drained

Cook frozen vegetables according to package directions, drain, and cool. In a large salad bowl, combine all ingredients except dressing, salt, pepper, and pimientos. Toss mixture lightly with dressing, season to taste, and garnish with pimientos.　*8 servings*

Layered Buffet Salad

6 cups torn iceberg lettuce
1 cup chopped celery
1 (16-oz.) can **GREEN GIANT® KITCHEN SLICED® Green Beans**, drained
4 hard cooked eggs, sliced
1 cup chopped green pepper
⅓ cup thinly sliced onion rings
1 (17-oz.) can **LE SUEUR® Early Peas**, drained
2 cups real mayonnaise
1 cup coarsely grated Cheddar cheese

In a large salad bowl layer the lettuce, celery, green beans, eggs, green pepper, onion and peas in order given. Spread the mayonnaise over the top of the salad; sprinkle with grated cheese. Cover well and let stand for 8 hours or overnight.　*Serves 8 to 10*

Andalusian Salad

1 small onion
1 crushed garlic clove
Grated peel ½ orange
1 tablespoon minced parsley
10 almonds, coarsely chopped
½ teaspoon cumin powder or curry powder
½ teaspoon salt
Freshly ground black pepper
½ cup **POMPEIAN Olive Oil**
¼ cup red wine vinegar
Mixed salad greens, about 6 cups

Mince onion. Combine with crushed garlic, orange peel, parsley, almonds, cumin or curry powder, salt and pepper. Add **POMPEIAN Olive Oil** and blend well, then add vinegar. Allow dressing to season for 30 minutes to 1 hour before using. Arrange salad greens in large salad bowl and add dressing at table, tossing gently but thoroughly to mix well.　*Serves 6*

CRISCO OIL

Caesar Salad

1 clove garlic, halved
¾ cup **CRISCO® Oil**
1 teaspoon salt
¼ teaspoon pepper
1 tablespoon Worcestershire sauce
2 cups toasted croutons
Romaine lettuce, about 3 quarts bite-size pieces
¼ cup Parmesan cheese
3 tablespoons lemon juice
2 tablespoons vinegar
1 egg, slightly beaten
10 to 12 anchovy fillets

Let garlic stand in **CRISCO® Oil** for several hours. Remove garlic. Combine ½ cup **CRISCO® Oil**, salt, pepper, and Worcestershire sauce. Heat the other ¼ cup **CRISCO® Oil** and stir in the toasted croutons; set aside.

Sprinkle bite-size pieces of lettuce with Parmesan cheese. Combine lemon juice, vinegar, and **CRISCO® Oil** mixture and pour over greens. Add egg to seasoned greens. Gently turn and toss salad until greens are coated with dressing and no trace of egg remains. Add croutons and toss lightly. Top with anchovy fillets. Serve at once.

Note: For a main-dish salad, add 1½ cups cooked roast beef strips, 1 cup cherry tomatoes, and 1 medium onion, separated into rings.

Cheez-It Caesar Salad

⅓ cup salad oil
3 tablespoons lemon juice
½ teaspoon salt
⅛ teaspoon pepper
1 small head chicory
1 small head romaine lettuce
1 small head escarole
16 **CHEEZ-IT® Crackers**
1 small garlic bud, halved
1 raw egg

Combine salad oil, lemon juice, salt and pepper in small bowl. Wash chicory, romaine and escarole, and remove any limp outer leaves. Break or cut greens into 2 inch pieces, discarding tough spines. Rub **CHEEZ-IT® Crackers** with surface of garlic. Also rub inside of a large wooden salad bowl with garlic. Arrange greens in garlic-rubbed bowl. Break the raw egg over the salad and add crackers, broken in half. Stir oil-lemon juice dressing to blend well; pour over salad and toss with salad fork and spoon until greens are well coated with egg and dressing.

Yield: 6 to 8 generous servings

Healthy Caesar Salad

1 small clove garlic, crushed
Caesar Salad Dressing*
2 heads romaine lettuce, torn into bite-size pieces (about 3 quarts)
Garlic Croutons**
¼ cup Parmesan cheese

Rub bottom of salad bowl with garlic. Add Caesar Salad Dressing. Add lettuce and Garlic Croutons; toss gently until greens are coated. Add cheese; toss again and serve immediately.

Makes 4 to 6 servings

*Caesar Salad Dressing

Place 1 small clove garlic, crushed in ⅓ cup **MAZOLA® Corn Oil**. Let stand several hours. Remove. In small bowl with whisk beat together garlic corn oil, 2 tablespoons lemon juice, 2 tablespoons water, 1 tablespoon white wine vinegar, 1 egg white, 1 teaspoon Worcestershire sauce, ¼ teaspoon salt and ¼ teaspoon pepper until well blended.

Makes about ⅔ cup

**Garlic Croutons

Place 1 small clove garlic, crushed, in ¼ cup **MAZOLA® Corn Oil**. Let stand several hours. Remove. In large skillet heat garlic corn oil over medium heat. Add 4 slices bread, crusts removed and cut into cubes; toss to coat. Place in shallow baking pan. Bake in 400°F oven 10 to 12 minutes or until golden brown.

Makes about 1 cup

Western Salad Bowl

½ lb. **WILSON® Bacon**
1 head romaine or iceberg lettuce
2 tomatoes, cut in wedges
1 cup shredded Cheddar cheese
3 green onions, sliced
¼ cup coarsely chopped ripe olives
Avocado Dressing*

Cook bacon until crisp. Drain and crumble. Remove outside leaves from lettuce and use to line a large shallow salad bowl. Chop remaining lettuce. Place on lettuce leaves. Arrange tomato wedges near edge of lettuce. Sprinkle cheese in a circle just inside the tomatoes. Follow with a circle of bacon, one of green onion and one of ripe olives. Leave about a 4″ space in the center. Chill until serving time. Spoon Avocado Dressing into center. If desired, sprinkle with bacon and green onion.

Makes 6 to 8 servings

*Avocado Dressing

Cut 1 large ripe avocado in half. Remove pit and peel. Mash until smooth. Stir in 1 tablespoon lemon juice, ½ cup dairy sour cream, ¼ teaspoon garlic salt, ¼ teaspoon salt, ⅛ teaspoon pepper and a dash ground red (cayenne) pepper. Refrigerate.

Roquefort Salad

¼ teaspoon chervil
¼ pound **ROQUEFORT**
¾ cup light cream
5 tablespoons lemon juice
½ teaspoon freshly ground black pepper
2 heads Romaine lettuce
BROWNBERRY® Onion and Garlic Croutons

Soak the chervil (if dried) in warm water 10 minutes. Drain. If fresh chervil is available, use 2 teaspoons. Mash the cheese and blend in the cream, lemon juice, pepper and chervil, until very smooth. Tear the lettuce into bite-sized pieces and pour the dressing over it. Add croutons at the last minute and toss until well coated.

Cheese-Capped Iceberg

1 package (8 oz) cream cheese, softened
¾ cup **BEST FOODS®/HELLMANN'S® Real Mayonnaise**
½ cup chopped pimiento-stuffed olives
2 tablespoons minced green onion
1 medium head iceberg lettuce
¼ cup catchup
2 teaspoons cider vinegar
¾ teaspoon chili powder
Dash hot pepper sauce

In small bowl with mixer at medium speed beat cream cheese until light and fluffy. Stir in ¼ cup **Real Mayonnaise**, olives and onion. Remove core from lettuce. Hollow out center leaving 1 inch shell. Fill with cheese mixture. Seal in plastic bag or aluminum foil. Stir together ½ cup **Real Mayonnaise** and remaining ingredients; cover. Chill lettuce and dressing overnight. Cut lettuce into 6 wedges; serve with dressing.

Makes 6 servings

Shades o' Green Salad

3 cups spinach (about)
4 stalks Pascal celery
½ green pepper
1 cucumber
½ head lettuce
2 tablespoons chopped chives
⅓ cup French dressing*
6 stuffed green olives
1 small avocado

Chill 6 individual salad bowls in refrigerator. Remove and discard tough stems, roots, and bruised leaves from the spinach. Wash, drain, and pat dry. Use part of the spinach to line the salad bowls. Set the remainder aside.

Cut into pieces or slices the celery, green pepper, and cucumber. Rinse, drain, and pat dry the lettuce. Tear lettuce and reserved spinach into pieces. Toss vegetables with lettuce, spinach, and chopped chives. Add French Dressing. Toss lightly to coat greens evenly.

Arrange individual portions of salad in bowls. Slice green olives. Rinse, peel, cut into halves lengthwise, remove pit, and slice the avocado. Garnish salad with avocado and olive slices.

Note: For a main-dish salad, add 1 pound fresh shrimp. Lightly toss shrimp with salad greens.

*French Dressing

¾ cup **CRISCO® Oil**
¼ cup lemon juice or cider vinegar
1 tablespoon sugar
¾ teaspoon salt
¼ teaspoon paprika
¼ teaspoon dry mustard
¼ teaspoon pepper

Combine the above ingredients in a screw-top jar. Cover tightly and shake vigorously to blend well. Store covered in refrigerator. Shake well before using.

About 1 cup

Flaming Salad

1½ lbs. fresh spinach
½ lb. diced bacon
½ cup wine vinegar
2 Tbsp. Worcestershire sauce
Juice of 1 lemon
½ cup sugar
½ cup **HIRAM WALKER Triple Sec**

Wash spinach and pat dry. Lightly brown bacon in small sauce pan. Drain all but 2 Tbsp. fat. Add vinegar, Worcestershire sauce, lemon juice and sugar. When sauce boils, pour over spinach. Add **Triple Sec** to pan, flame and pour flaming over spinach.

Serves 6 to 8

Spinach-Cheddar Toss

1 **DARIGOLD Egg**, hard cooked and sliced
½ cup olives, sliced
1 small head lettuce, torn into pieces
2 cups torn spinach leaves
1 cup (4 oz.) **DARIGOLD Red Boy Cheese**, shredded
4 slices bacon, cooked crisp, drained and crumbled
½ cup Light Style Salad Dressing*, heated

Pour heated Light Style Dressing over the ingredients. Toss and serve immediately.

Makes 6 servings

*Light Style Salad Dressing
(Low Calorie)

1 pkg. salad dressing mix (use one that calls for 1 cup mayonnaise and 1 cup buttermilk)
½ pint **DARIGOLD Sour Cream**
3 Tbsp. **DARIGOLD Powdered Buttermilk**
1 cup water

To make a low calorie dressing, substitute **DARIGOLD Sour Cream** and **DARIGOLD Powdered Buttermilk** in a package mix that calls for mayonnaise and fresh buttermilk. Blend all ingredients listed above together. *Makes 1 pint dressing*

Calories: Approximately 18 calories per tablespoon.

Best Foods® HELLMANN'S®
Spinach Salad

3 quarts (1 lb) washed, drained and torn spinach leaves
⅓ cup sliced green onion
⅔ cup **MAZOLA® Corn Oil**
½ cup **BEST FOODS®/HELLMANN'S® Real Mayonnaise**
½ cup wine vinegar
1 clove garlic, minced
3 hard cooked eggs, sliced

In large salad bowl place spinach and onion. Stir together corn oil, real mayonnaise, vinegar and garlic. Pour half of mixture onto spinach; toss. Place egg slices on top of salad. Serve with remaining dressing.

Makes 6 to 8 servings

Lemon-Zesty Spinach Salad

1 lb. fresh spinach
1 16-oz can Chinese vegetables without celery, drained and rinsed
⅔ cup salad oil
¼ cup sugar
¼ cup catsup
¼ cup **MINUTE MAID® 100% Pure Lemon Juice**
¼ cup Worcestershire sauce
2 Tbsp. coarsely chopped onion, or 1 Tbsp. instant minced onion
6 slices crisp bacon, crumbled
6 large fresh mushrooms, sliced

Wash spinach thoroughly, drain and tear into bite-size pieces. Combine spinach and Chinese vegetables in a large bowl, cover tightly and chill. Combine next 6 ingredients in an electric blender and blend well; store in refrigerator. At serving time, pour dressing over vegetables, add sliced mushrooms, and sprinkle bacon on top; toss lightly.
Yield 6-8 servings

SUE BEE HONEY

Hawaiian Spinach Salad

1 pound spinach
1 can (15½-oz.) cut yellow wax beans, drained
1 can (15½-oz.) pineapple chunks, drained
½ cup sugar
1 cup **SUE BEE® Honey**
1 teaspoon grated onion
6 tablespoons tarragon vinegar
3 tablespoons lemon juice
1 cup salad oil
1 teaspoon dry mustard
1 teaspoon paprika
¼ teaspoon salt
2 teaspoons poppy seeds
1 teaspoon curry powder

Wash spinach and tear into bite-sized pieces. Combine with beans and pineapple; chill. Combine remaining ingredients in a jar and shake thoroughly. (Dressing keeps indefinitely in refrigerator.) When ready to serve, pour dressing over spinach salad.
Makes six to eight servings

Hungarian Cucumbers

2 large cucumbers
1 large onion
Ice water
Salt
¼ cup **POMPEIAN Olive Oil**
¼ cup tarragon vinegar
1 cup sour cream
Dash cayenne
Parsley (garnish)

Peel cucumbers, score with fork, slice thin as possible. Slice onion same way. Place alternate layers in shallow dish, sprinkling each layer with salt. Cover with ice water and chill 2 to 3 hours. Drain, rinse with running water, drain again. Mix **POMPEIAN Olive Oil** and vinegar, pour over vegetables, marinate 2 to 3 hours. Drain. Arrange on platter, alternating cucumber and onion slices. Pour on sour cream. Sprinkle with cayenne. Garnish with parsley.
Serves 6

Lipton.

Scandinavian Cucumber Salad

½ cup **LIPTON®** California Dip*
1 tablespoon vinegar
1 teaspoon sugar
½ teaspoon salt
¼ teaspoon dill weed
2 large cucumbers, thinly sliced

In medium bowl, combine all ingredients; chill.
About 4 servings

VARIATION:

Substitute raw cauliflowerets for the cucumbers.

*Lipton® California Dip

In small bowl, blend 1 envelope **LIPTON® Onion Soup Mix** with 2 cups (16 oz.) sour cream; chill.

Dilled Cucumber Slices
(Low Calorie/Low Cholesterol)

3 cucumbers peeled and sliced paper thin
½ teaspoon salt
¼ cup white wine vinegar
¼ cup water
2 teaspoons **SWEETLITE™ Fructose**
2 teaspoons dill weed

Place the sliced cucumbers in a shallow non-metal bowl and sprinkle them with salt. Cover the cucumbers and put them in the refrigerator for at least two hours. Drain the cucumbers thoroughly. Mix all remaining ingredients together and pour over the cucumbers. Chill well before serving. Dilled Cucumber Slices are excellent with cold seafood.
Makes 6 servings

Each serving contains approximately:
¼ fruit exchange
10 calories
0 mg cholesterol

Oriental Cucumber Salad

2 medium-size cucumbers, peeled and seeded
2 teaspoons salt
¼ cup distilled white vinegar
1 tablespoon sugar
1 tablespoon water
1½ teaspoons **KIKKOMAN Soy Sauce**
¼ teaspoon grated fresh ginger root *OR* ⅛ teaspoon ground ginger

Cut cucumbers into thin slices; place in bowl and sprinkle with salt. Let stand at room temperature 1 to 2 hours. Drain and squeeze out excess liquid. Combine vinegar, sugar, water, soy sauce and ginger in serving bowl; add cucumbers and mix well. Chill thoroughly before serving.
Makes 4 servings

Diet for Dilettantes

(Low Calorie)

ICEBERG Lettuce leaves, crisped
1½ cups shredded ICEBERG Lettuce
8 ounce cup plain whole milk yogurt, well chilled*
½ ounce caviar, black or red
1 tablespoon minced onion
1 teaspoon sieved egg yolk
1 or 2 parsley sprigs
Lemon wedge

Core, rinse and thoroughly drain lettuce; chill in disposable plastic bag or plastic crisper. Line serving plate with lettuce leaves; fill with shredded lettuce. Pierce bottom of yogurt cup and invert contents onto lettuce. Yogurt should be very cold to hold cup shape. Not all brands stand tall so experiment, if necessary. Top with caviar, onion and egg. Garnish with parsley and lemon. Serve with unsalted Melba toast and Champagne.

Makes 1 serving, about 250 calories

*8 ounces low-fat yogurt contain about 130 calories as compared to 145 calories for whole milk yogurt above.

Favorite recipe from the **California Iceberg Lettuce Commission**

TABASCO®

Very Green Salad

2 packages (10 ounces each) frozen green peas
¼ cup chopped scallions
1 cup sliced celery
1 head Boston lettuce

Cook peas according to package directions, drain, and mix with scallions, celery, and ¼ cup Green Mayonnaise*. Cover and chill until ready to serve. To serve, separate lettuce leaves into cups and place on 6 salad plates. Spoon salad into lettuce cups and serve with remaining mayonnaise.   *6 servings*

*Green Mayonnaise

1 cup water
10 fresh spinach leaves
1 tablespoon chopped chives
¼ cup watercress leaves
¼ cup chopped parsley
1 teaspoon dried leaf tarragon
1 egg
¼ teaspoon dry mustard
½ teaspoon salt
1 tablespoon lemon juice
½ teaspoon TABASCO® Pepper Sauce
1 cup salad oil

In medium saucepan combine water, spinach leaves, chives, watercress, parsley and tarragon. Place over medium heat, bring to a boil and boil 3 minutes. Drain well and turn into container of electric blender. Add egg, dry mustard, salt, lemon juice and **TABASCO®**. Cover and process until smooth. Remove cover and while blender is running, very gradually add oil in a thin steady stream or 1 tablespoon at a time, continuing to blend until all oil is absorbed. Chill.

About 1¼ cups
(Continued)

56

Note: To make Green Mayonnaise with commercial mayonnaise, measure 1 cup mayonnaise into small bowl and blend in 1 tablespoon lemon juice, ¼ teaspoon dried mustard, ½ teaspoon **TABASCO® Pepper Sauce**, ¼ cup chopped watercress, ¼ cup chopped parsley, 1 tablespoon chopped chives and ½ teaspoon dried tarragon.

Hot Wilted Lettuce Salad

2 medium size heads lettuce or equal amount leaf lettuce
1 small diced onion
4 strips bacon
2 Tbsp. FIGARO Fresh Garlic Vinegar
1 Tbsp. sugar

Tear lettuce in large pieces. Fry bacon crisp and break up in small pieces. Mix bacon and onions through lettuce. Add **FIGARO Garlic Vinegar** and sugar to drippings from bacon, heat well and pour over lettuce. Serve while hot.   *Enough for six*

Wilted Lettuce

4 cups leaf lettuce
3 tablespoons PURITAN® Oil
⅓ cup cider vinegar
3 tablespoons bacon bits
2 tablespoons sugar
1 teaspoon salt
¼ teaspoon pepper

Tear lettuce into pieces. Bring remaining ingredients to a boil. Reduce heat and simmer 2 to 3 minutes. Pour hot mixture over lettuce in a bowl and toss to coat evenly.   *4 servings*

VARIATION:

Hot Slaw

Follow above recipe but substitute 4 cups shredded cabbage for lettuce.

Ratatouille Relish

¼ cup olive oil
1 medium eggplant, coarsely chopped
1 onion, chopped
1 can (28 ounces) Italian-style tomatoes, drained
¼ cup red wine vinegar
2 teaspoons sugar
½ teaspoon salt
¼ teaspoon pepper
10 pimiento-stuffed green olives, sliced

Heat oil in large skillet until hot. Stir in eggplant and onion. Cook, stirring constantly, until onion is transparent and eggplant is tender. Stir in remaining ingredients. Simmer, uncovered, 15 minutes. Cover and refrigerate up to 24 hours. Serve at room temperature.   *Makes about 5 cups*

Favorite recipe from the **California Iceberg Lettuce Commission**

Chopped Eggplant Salad

1 large eggplant
¾ teaspoon salt
3 tablespoons oil
1 medium onion, diced
2 tablespoons white vinegar
1 to 2 tablespoons sugar
½ tablespoon garlic powder
SUNSHINE® Crackers

Core eggplant, and wrap in aluminum foil. Bake at 350°F. for 45 minutes, or until soft. Cool and peel skin. Chop eggplant, salt, oil, onion, vinegar, sugar, and garlic powder. Refrigerate for one to two hours. Season again if needed. Serve with assortment of **SUNSHINE® Crackers**. *Yield: 6 servings*

Summer Salad Supreme

2 cups chopped tomato
1 cup thick sliced cucumber
1 can (3 oz.) **BinB® Sliced Mushrooms**, undrained
3 tablespoons vegetable oil
3 tablespoons wine or cider vinegar
1 clove garlic, minced
1 teaspoon salt
Dash pepper
Lettuce
3 tablespoons blue cheese, crumbled (optional)

Place tomato, cucumber and mushrooms, including buttery broth in bowl. Combine remaining ingredients except cheese and lettuce and pour over vegetables. Chill several hours. To serve, sprinkle with cheese and place on lettuce.

Makes 3¼ cups or 4 to 6 servings

Oriental Broccoli and Bean Sprout Salad

2 lbs. fresh broccoli
½ lb. fresh mushrooms, cleaned
1 can (16 oz.) **LA CHOY® Bean Sprouts**, rinsed and drained
⅓ cup cider vinegar
⅓ cup salad oil (not olive oil)
2 teaspoons catsup
1 teaspoon salt
Freshly ground black pepper to taste

Cut broccoli florets from stalks. Pare stalks and cut into ¼-inch slices. Cook broccoli stalks in boiling water 1 minute; rinse under cold water and drain. Cook florets 2 minutes in boiling salted water; rinse with cold water and drain. Combine cooked broccoli with mushrooms and bean sprouts. Blend remaining ingredients, pour over vegetables, mixing well. Marinate 1 hour in refrigerator. Serve on crisp lettuce leaves. *8 servings*

Chinese Garden Salad

½ cup vinegar
¼ cup water
¼ cup sugar
4 teaspoons salt
1½ teaspoons monosodium glutamate
¼ teaspoon minced garlic
¼ teaspoon black pepper
2 tablespoons diced red pepper
2 tablespoons finely diced onion
2 cans (1 lb. each) **LA CHOY® Fancy Bean Sprouts**, drained
¼ cup vegetable oil

Heat water and vinegar in sauce pan. Stir in sugar, salt, monosodium glutamate and garlic. Pour seasoned mixture over Bean Sprouts, peppers and onions. Stir; let cool. Add vegetable oil, toss lightly and serve. Chill for best results. *Yield: 6 Servings*

Cool Corn Salad

¼ cup commercial sour cream
¼ cup mayonnaise
1 tablespoon prepared mustard
2 teaspoons white vinegar
1 teaspoon sugar
¼ teaspoon salt
⅛ teaspoon pepper
1 can (17 ounces) **STOKELY'S FINEST® Whole Kernel Golden Corn**, drained
1 jar (2 ounces) **STOKELY'S FINEST® Sliced Pimientos**, drained and diced
2 carrots, peeled and grated
½ cup diced onion

In medium-size bowl, make dressing by combining sour cream, mayonnaise, mustard, vinegar, sugar, salt, and pepper. Add remaining ingredients and toss to blend. Cover and refrigerate at least 1 hour. *4 to 6 servings*

Salad Rouge

1 can (4 oz.) **ORTEGA® Whole (or Sliced) Pimientos**
1½ cups fresh mushrooms, sliced
¾ cup black pitted olives, sliced
½ cup pine nuts (or sliced walnuts)
1 can (4 oz.) tiny shrimp (optional)
1 cup prepared Italian salad dressing
6-8 lettuce leaves (Bibb lettuce is preferred)

Drain and chop pimientos; place in glass dish with mushrooms, olives, nuts and drained shrimp. Pour dressing over vegetables, nuts, and shrimp; stir to coat. Place in refrigerator at least 2-3 hours (8 hours preferred). To serve, remove with slotted spoon to drain excess marinade and place in lettuce cups on salad plates. Garnish with additional strips of pimientos or curly parsley. An unusual salad idea which can be served as an appetizer as well.

Serves 6-8

Pea and Cheese Salad

2 cups peas (canned or fresh cooked)
¼ lb. **CHEEZ-OLA®** or **COUNT DOWN®**
½ cup sliced celery
⅓ cup mayonnaise (safflower or corn oil mayonnaise)

Chill the peas thoroughly in their liquid, then drain off juice. Dice cheese about the same size as the peas. Combine peas with remaining ingredients and toss gently. Serve in lettuce cups.

5 servings

DANNON® YOGURT

Salad and Dressing "Maison"

Yogurt over chopped vegetables in season—celery, radishes, peppers, cucumbers—is wonderfully refreshing. Don't forget salt and pepper. Try this "do it yourself" vegetable yogurt in your own home.

For a fascinating dressing with a decidedly different accent, mix one cup of **DANNON® Plain Yogurt** with a half cup of commercial mayonnaise or Russian dressing; for use over lettuce or topping over fresh fruit salad.

Tomato Baskets

4 large red tomatoes, ripe but firm
1 (16 oz.) can **VEG-ALL® Mixed Vegetables**, drained
¾ cup cooked rice
3 tsp. minced onion
3 tsp. mayonnaise
1 egg, hard cooked, and chopped
4 large pepper rings
4 leaves of lettuce
4 black olives
Season to taste

Cut off top of tomatoes to form basket, spoon pulp from center of tomatoes and chop. Combine chopped tomato with **VEG-ALL®**, rice, onion, and mayonnaise. Spoon into tomato basket.

To serve, place each basket in a green pepper ring that has been placed on a lettuce leaf. Sprinkle some chopped egg on each, and top with black olive.

Serves 4

Middle Eastern Yogurt Salad

2 medium tomatoes, sliced thin
1 medium cucumber, sliced wafer thin
1 cup plain yogurt
Salt to taste
2 tablespoons **HOLLAND HOUSE® White Cooking Wine**
1 teaspoon white wine vinegar
2 scallions, chopped

Rub cucumbers with salt; rinse and drain. Rinse and drain again after 10 minutes. Mix wine, vinegar and yogurt together in a large bowl. Add tomatoes and cucumbers. Toss lightly. Sprinkle with chopped onion. Chill.

Serves 2 to 4

Irish Mist® Liqueur
Limerick Salad

¼ cup **IRISH MIST®**
¾ cup oil
¼ cup red wine vinegar
3 tablespoons **GREY POUPON® Dijon Mustard**
2 tablespoons honey
6 small tomatoes, peeled and sliced*
1 small red onion, thinly sliced
Bibb or Boston lettuce
Toasted sesame seeds

Combine **IRISH MIST®**, oil, vinegar, mustard and honey. Set aside. Arrange tomato and onion slices on bed of lettuce. Spoon dressing over salad. Sprinkle with sesame seeds.   *Serves 6*

*To peel tomatoes drop into boiling water for 30 seconds. Remove and peel skin. Core tomatoes and cut into thin slices.

Tomatoes With Avocado Dressing

Dressing:
1 ripe **CALAVO® Avocado**
⅓ cup mayonnaise
1 tablespoon lemon or lime juice
1 tablespoon onion juice
Dash of Worcestershire
Salt to taste

3 large tomatoes
Lettuce leaves
Chopped chives

DRESSING:
Put avocado in blender or food processor. Mix with mayonnaise, add lemon or lime juice, onion juice, Worcestershire and salt.

Peel 3 large tomatoes, slice and arrange on lettuce leaves. Pour dressing over tomatoes and sprinkle with chopped chives.

Serves 4

Garden Stuffed Tomatoes
(Low Calorie/Low Cholesterol/Low Fat)

4 medium tomatoes, whole
1 Tbsp. corn oil margarine
½ cup chopped onion
¼ cup chopped green pepper
½ cup celery
1 tsp. basil
1 tsp. oregano
4 tsp. **ESTEE® Granulated Fructose**
4 slices low-fat American Cheese

Preheat oven to 350°F. Cut off tops from tomatoes. Scoop out pulp, leaving shell intact. Save pulp. Melt margarine in frying pan. Add chopped tomato pulp, onions, celery, and green pepper. Cook until tender. Add seasonings and **ESTEE® Fructose**, simmer 5 minutes. Fill tomatoes with cooked vegetable mixture. Arrange stuffed tomatoes in ungreased baking pan and bake, uncovered, for 25 minutes. Remove pan from oven and top each tomato with a slice of low-fat American Cheese. Bake 10 minutes more to melt cheese.   *Makes 4 servings, 1 tomato per serving*

NUTRITION INFORMATION

Calories	Carbohydrates	Protein	Fat	Cholesterol	Sodium
115	14g	7g	4g	7 mg	351*mg

DIABETIC EXCHANGE INFORMATION

Meat	Vegetables
1 (low fat)	2

*For sodium-restricted diets: Omit low-fat American Cheese and sprinkle each tomato with 1 tsp. grated Parmesan cheese. One tomato with Parmesan cheese contains 55 milligrams sodium.

Zucchini-Stuffed Tomatoes

1 cup (4-ounces) **P & R Rings**, uncooked
6 to 8 medium tomatoes
½ cup grated zucchini
1 cup cottage cheese
½ teaspoon basil
¼ teaspoon salt
⅛ teaspoon pepper

Cook Rings according to package directions; drain well. Cool. (Rinse with cold water to cool quickly; drain well.) Remove core from tomatoes; scoop pulp from tomatoes leaving a ½-inch shell. Combine ½ cup chopped tomato pulp, zucchini, cottage cheese, basil, salt and pepper in medium bowl; add cooled Rings and toss. Fill tomato shells; chill. Serve on lettuce leaves with wheat crackers, if desired.   *6 to 8 servings*

VARIATION:

Top tomatoes with shredded mozzarella cheese; place under broiler several minutes until cheese melts. Serve immediately.

Tomatoes Vinaigrette

3 to 4 tomatoes, sliced
1 cup **PURITAN® Oil**
⅓ cup wine vinegar
2 teaspoons oregano
1 teaspoon sugar
1 teaspoon salt
1 teaspoon dried parsley flakes
½ teaspoon pepper
½ teaspoon dry mustard
2 cloves garlic, crushed
6 green onions, minced

Arrange tomato slices in square glass baking dish. Combine remaining ingredients, except green onions, and pour over tomatoes. Cover, chill at least 2 to 3 hours, basting occasionally. Before serving, top with minced green onions.   *6 servings*

Gazpacho Garden Salad

½ cup vegetable oil
⅓ cup **REALEMON® Lemon Juice From Concentrate**
2 cloves garlic, finely chopped
1½ teaspoons salt
¼ teaspoon pepper
1 medium green pepper, seeded and diced
2 medium, firm tomatoes, diced
1 medium cucumber, peeled, seeded and diced
½ cup sliced green onion

In 1-pint jar with tight-fitting lid, combine oil, **REALEMON®**, garlic, salt and pepper; shake well. In narrow 1-quart glass container, layer ½ each of the green pepper, tomato, cucumber and onion; repeat layering with remaining vegetables. Pour dressing over salad. Chill 4 hours to blend flavors.   *Makes 8 servings*

California Mushroom Salad

2 cups sliced **DOLE® Fresh Mushrooms**
½ cup Italian-style dressing
1 large tomato
1 cup julienne-cut green pepper
1½ quarts torn crisp salad greens
2 oz. Greek feta cheese, crumbled

In a large salad bowl, toss sliced mushrooms with Italian-style dressing. Coarsely chop tomato and toss with green pepper and mushrooms. Let stand 5 minutes. Add salad greens to vegetables, mixing well. Sprinkle feta cheese on top to serve.   *Makes 6 to 8 servings*

VARIATIONS:

Marinate sliced **DOLE® Fresh Mushrooms**, artichoke hearts and ripe olives in an olive oil and lemon juice marinade with garlic and oregano. Drain marinade, toss vegetables and spoon them onto individual salad plates. Sprinkle with Greek Feta cheese.

Tear Romaine lettuce into bite size pieces; combine with sliced **DOLE® Fresh Mushrooms** and chopped green onions. Toss with Italian dressing and sprinkle with grated Parmesan cheese.

Marinate sliced **DOLE® Fresh Mushrooms** and sliced cauliflowerettes in white wine vinegar, salad oil, garlic salt, rosemary and black pepper. Drain marinade. Arrange vegetables on salad plates lined with crisp salad greens. Top with chopped green onions.

Lindsay® Frenchy Ripe Olive Salad

For an attractive and somewhat different salad, marinate in French dressing, sliced ripe tomatoes, sliced green onions and **LINDSAY® Sliced Ripe Olives**. Chill well. Drain and serve on crisp lettuce leaves.

THE CHRISTIAN BROTHERS®
Salad Skewers

1 box cherry tomatoes
½ lb. fresh mushrooms
½ head cauliflower, broken into flowerets
2 green peppers, cut into squares
1 cup ripe olives
⅔ cup oil
½ cup **THE CHRISTIAN BROTHERS®** Riesling
   Wine
3 Tbsp. lemon juice
½ tsp. salt
1 clove garlic, crushed
¼ tsp. pepper

Put vegetables in container with tight fitting lid. Combine oil, wine, lemon juice, salt, garlic and pepper; pour over vegetables. Marinate until serving time. For each serving, place assorted marinated vegetables on wooden skewer.   *Serves 6*

Mazola®
Marinaded Vegetables With Dressing

2 pounds assorted fresh vegetables, cooked, such as
   green beans, cauliflowerets, broccoli flowerets and
   thinly sliced zucchini
1 cup **MAZOLA®** Corn Oil
⅓ cup white wine vinegar
1 clove garlic, minced
1 teaspoon salt
1 teaspoon sugar
¼ teaspoon pepper
1 cup plain yogurt
3 tablespoons reserved marinade
2 tablespoons chopped parsley
¼ teaspoon dried oregano leaves

Place vegetables in large shallow dish. In small bowl stir together corn oil, vinegar, garlic, salt, sugar and pepper. Pour over vegetables. Cover; refrigerate overnight. Drain vegetables, reserving marinade. Arrange vegetables on serving platter. In small bowl stir in 3 tablespoons marinade into yogurt. Add parsley and oregano. Serve dressing with vegetables.   *Makes 6 servings*

Note: Keep remaining marinade in a jar with tight-fitting cover in refrigerator. ¼ teaspoon curry may be substituted for oregano.

claussen
Sauerkraut Salad

1 jar (2 lb.) **CLAUSSEN Sauerkraut**, drained
1 cup sugar*
1 cup white vinegar
3 ribs celery, chopped
2 medium green peppers, chopped
1 medium onion, chopped
½ (1 can, 1 lb.) pitted ripe olives, sliced

In large bowl combine all ingredients. Cover and chill several hours or overnight.   *Makes 10 (½ cup) servings*

*To further reduce calories, an artificial sugar replacement can be substituted. Use as package directs for equivalency to granulated sugar or to taste.

IMPERIAL Pure Cane SUGAR®
Sweet and Sauerkraut Salad

¾ cup **IMPERIAL Granulated Sugar**
¾ teaspoon salt
½ cup cider vinegar
¼ cup vegetable oil
½ cup onion, chopped
½ cup green pepper, chopped
½ cup celery, chopped
1 (4 ounce) jar diced pimiento
1 cup unpeeled apple, diced
2 cups (1 pound can) sauerkraut, rinsed and drained

Combine **IMPERIAL Granulated Sugar**, salt, vinegar and oil to make dressing. Combine remaining ingredients and toss well with dressing. Chill thoroughly and drain before serving. Dressing may be saved and used again.   *Serves 8*

Vegetable & Fruit Combos

Cucumber Fruit Salad With Peanut Dressing*

1 large **CALAVO®-BURNAC EUROPEAN**
   Cucumber—sliced thinly
1 small can well drained mandarin orange segments (or
   fresh orange slices may be used)
1 banana, sliced
1 avocado, sliced
Shredded coconut (optional)
Butter lettuce

Arrange cucumber, avocado and fruits on a lettuce-lined platter. Drizzle dressing over salad.   *Serves 4*

*Peanut Dressing

½ cup peanuts
1 tsp. Champagne vinegar
⅛ tsp. curry
¼ cup mayonnaise
¼ cup sour cream
¼ cup chutney

Place all in blender or food processor. Blend until smooth.
      Makes approximately 1¼ cups

Fruit, Avocado & Cheese Salad

1 medium head Boston lettuce
1 clove garlic
2 grapefruits
1 large navel orange
2 medium avocados
1 container (15 oz.) **MIGLIORE® Ricotta**
3 tablespoons lemon juice
3 tablespoons olive oil
1 teaspoon sugar
¾ teaspoon salt
Dash of pepper

Wash and drain lettuce and tear into bite-size pieces. Rub inside of large salad bowl with garlic. Add lettuce. Peel grapefruit and orange; cut into sections. Cut avocados in half lengthwise, remove pits and peel. Slice avocados and sprinkle with 2 tablespoons lemon juice. Arrange fruit and avocados on lettuce in sunburst fashion. Pile cheese in center. Mix together olive oil, remaining lemon juice, sugar, salt and pepper. Pour over salad.

Avocado-Orange Toss

6 ounces spinach, torn into bite-size pieces
2 oranges, pared and sectioned
1 avocado, sliced
2 green onions (with tops), thinly sliced
Lemon Dressing*
BAC★OS® Imitation Bacon

Toss spinach, oranges, avocado and onions with Lemon Dressing. Sprinkle with imitation bacon.   *6 to 8 servings*

*Lemon Dressing

¼ cup vegetable oil
2 tablespoons lemon juice
¼ teaspoon salt
¼ teaspoon dried tarragon leaves

Shake all ingredients in tightly covered container.

Cream Cheese and Avocado Salad

2 **CALAVO® Avocados** cut in half
1 (3 oz.) package cream cheese
1 tablespoon black olives sliced
2 tablespoons pimiento chopped
3 tablespoons Italian salad peppers chopped
Lemon juice

Add 1 teaspoon vinegar from Italian peppers to cream cheese and mix well in a food processor or blender. Add pimientos, peppers and black olives. Peel, seed and cut the avocados in half. Coat

with lemon juice. Fill the cavity with cream cheese mixture. Refrigerate for 1 hour. Serve on lettuce leaves.   *Serves 4*

Avocado Surprise Salad

2 medium avocados
2 oranges
1 large grapefruit (or 1 11-oz. can grapefruit sections, drained)
1 head lettuce, washed and crisped
1 can (4 oz.) **ORTEGA® Sliced Pimientos**
6 black pitted olives, sliced
1 can (7 oz.) **ORTEGA® Green Chile Salsa**

Peel, seed, and slice avocados, oranges and grapefruit. Alternate sections of fruits on individual plates lined with leaves of crisp lettuce (lettuce can also be shredded for easier eating). Garnish with strips of pimientos and black olives. Serve salsa in separate dish for salad dressing. You'll find the salsa a natural for salad dressing and a perfect match for avocados in particular.
          Serves 4-6

Caviar-Stuffed Avocados

1 pkg. (3 oz.) cream cheese, softened
¼ cup mayonnaise or salad dressing
½ cup minced celery
2 tsp. lemon juice
Few drops **TABASCO®**
2 ripe avocados
4 Tbsp. (2 oz.) **ROMANOFF® Caviar***
Crisp salad greens

Into cream cheese, blend mayonnaise, celery, lemon juice and **TABASCO®**. Halve avocados length-wise. Remove pits; peel. Brush with additional lemon juice. Set aside one tablespoon caviar. Fold remainder into cheese mixture. Use to fill hollows of avocados. Arrange on greens. Garnish with reserved caviar.
          Makes 4 servings

***ROMANOFF® Red Salmon Caviar** suggested.

Roquefort Avocado Salad Bowl

1 head lettuce, shredded
French dressing
ROQUEFORT Cheese
3 hard-cooked eggs
1 large avocado
Garlic

Rub salad bowl with garlic, discard garlic, and crumble in the **ROQUEFORT Cheese** (1 thin slice). Add shredded lettuce and egg sliced in thick rounds, with the avocado in thin, match-like strips. Pour in freshly made French dressing and toss lightly with salad fork and spoon. Serve well chilled.

Favorite recipe from the **Roquefort Association, Inc.**

Avocado Citrus Salad

1 large grapefruit or 1 cup drained canned grapefruit
  sections
2 oranges
3 cups mixed salad greens
1 cup green grapes or canned, sliced pears
2 California avocados
¼ cup walnuts
1 cup sour cream or yogurt
½ teaspoon dill weed

Section grapefruit and oranges. Place salad greens in bottom of
large salad bowl. Add grapefruit and orange sections and grapes.
Halve, peel and slice avocados. Arrange avocado slices over top of
salad in spin wheel fashion. Mound walnuts in center of bowl.
Blend sour cream with dill weed, serve with salad.

Makes 6 to 8 servings

Favorite recipe from the **California Avocado Commission**

Sweet Potato Fruit Salad

1 No. 3 Squat **TAYLOR'S** Sweet Potatoes
2 firm bananas
2 red apples
2 cups seedless grapes

Cube potatoes. Prepare fruits and mix with potatoes by tossing
lightly together. Serve on crisp lettuce with a tart-sweet dressing: 1
cup mayonnaise mixed with 1 tablespoon honey and 1 tablespoon
lemon juice. A sweetened oil and vinegar dressing is good with
this salad also.

Leafy Greens and Tropical Fruit Salad Bar

4 cups leaf lettuce
1 cup curly endive
1 cup escarole
⅓ cup vinegar
¼ cup lime juice
¾ cup sugar
1 teaspoon salt
1 teaspoon dry mustard
1 teaspoon celery seed
1 teaspoon paprika
1 cup salad oil
½ teaspoon grated onion
1 fresh pineapple, pared and diced
3 oranges, pared and sectioned
1 large banana, peeled and sliced
Flaked coconut

Wash greens; drain and tear into bite-size pieces. Store in plastic
bag in refrigerator. To make dressing, heat vinegar and lime juice
to boiling. Combine dry ingredients; add to hot mixture; stir till
sugar dissolves. Add oil and onion. Beat with rotary beater till
thoroughly mixed and slightly thickened. Chill.

  Place torn mixed salad greens in large shallow bowl. Arrange
fruit along side. To keep bananas bright, dip in lemon juice mixed
with a little water. Sprinkle flaked coconut over fruit. Serve with
dressing.

6 to 8 servings

Favorite recipe from the **Leafy Greens Council**

Mandarin Bacon Salad

½ head lettuce, bite size pieces
¼ head romaine, bite size pieces
6 slices **RATH® BLACK HAWK Bacon**, fried and
  crumbled
2 green onions, thinly sliced
1 small zucchini
1 11-oz. can mandarin orange segments, drained
¼ cup sliced almonds

Toss together first 6 ingredients; mix with dressing*. Just before
serving, add one 11-oz. can mandarin orange segments, drained.
Top with ¼ cup sliced almonds, slightly toasted.

*Dressing

¼ cup vegetable oil
2 Tbsp. sugar
2 Tbsp. vinegar
½ tsp. salt
Dash red pepper sauce

Mix well, add to greens as desired.

Chiquita® Banana Orange Melody Salad

1 medium head romaine lettuce, torn into pieces
4 **CHIQUITA® Bananas**, sliced
2 oranges, sectioned
½ cup halved pitted dates
½ cup coarsely chopped walnuts

In salad bowl, arrange lettuce, **CHIQUITA® Bananas**, oranges
and dates; toss with your favorite dressing and add walnuts.

Yield: Approximately 6 servings

Crisp Liteline Salad

1 can (16 oz.) **DEL MONTE Lite Sliced Pears**
¾ cup oil
3 Tbsp. lemon juice
1 Tbsp. chopped parsley
1 tsp. Dijon mustard
1 clove garlic, crushed
1 tsp. basil
1 tsp. dill weed
5 cups shredded red cabbage
3 green onions, sliced
1 cup tiny cooked shrimp
1 avocado, sliced

Drain fruit reserving liquid for other recipe uses. Thoroughly blend oil with lemon juice, parsley, mustard, garlic, basil and dill. Toss cabbage and onions with half the dressing. Arrange on individual serving plates with sliced pears, avocado and shrimp. Serve with remaining dressing.   *5 servings*

Key Salad

½ avocado pear
1 grapefruit
½ bunch curly endive
1 bunch watercress
1 small yellow onion
1 clove garlic
6 tablespoons olive oil
1 teaspoon sugar
1 teaspoon salt
1 teaspoon paprika
2 tablespoons **DUBONNET Blanc**

Peel grapefruit and section. Peel and slice onion very thin. Peel and slice avocado. Tear endive into pieces two or three inches long. Combine all remaining ingredients except watercress and blend by shaking vigorously in jar with screw top or bottle. Mix endive, onion, watercress and grapefruit sections. Add avocado last as it must be handled carefully. Remove garlic from dressing and pour over salad, tossing gently.

Peachtree Salad

⅔ cup salad oil
⅓ cup **HEINZ Wine Vinegar**
1 clove garlic, split
1 teaspoon sugar
½ teaspoon salt
⅛ teaspoon pepper
8 cups torn salad greens, chilled
1 cup finely chopped parsley
1 cup sliced fresh or canned peaches
½ cup broken pecans

Combine first 6 ingredients in jar. Cover; shake vigorously. Chill to blend flavors. Remove garlic and shake again before tossing with salad greens, parsley, peaches and nuts.
                              Makes 8 servings (about 8 cups)

ᵀᴴᴱ CHRISTIAN BROTHERS®

Brandy Fiesta Salad

6 slices (1-inch thick) fresh pineapple, halved, peeled and cored
3 oranges, peeled and sliced
⅔ cup **THE CHRISTIAN BROTHERS® Brandy**
⅓ cup sugar
¼ cup water
¼ teaspoon salt
¼ cup white wine vinegar
2 cups shredded green cabbage
2 cups shredded red cabbage
Cilantro or watercress sprigs

Combine pineapple and orange slices in bowl; set aside. In 1-quart saucepan combine brandy, sugar, water and salt. Bring to boiling, stirring. Simmer 5 minutes. Remove from heat. Stir in vinegar. Pour over fruits. Cover and chill several hours, tossing occasionally. Mound cabbage in serving bowl. Arrange fruits over cabbage. Drizzle with brandy mixture. Garnish with cilantro.
                              Makes 6 servings

SUN-MAID® RAISINS

Carrot Raisin Salad

½ cup **SUN-MAID® Raisins**
2 cups grated carrot
1 (8¾ ounce) can pineapple tidbits
⅓ cup mayonnaise
1 tablespoon lemon juice
¼ teaspoon salt
Salad greens

Combine **SUN-MAID® Raisins**, carrot and drained pineapple. Blend in mayonnaise, lemon juice and salt. Serve on crisp salad greens.   *Makes 4 to 6 servings*

Fruit Salads

Health Salad

1 cup diced apples
1 cup diced celery
1 cup grated carrot
1 cup raisins
1 cup sharp Cheddar cheese, grated
1 cup pineapple chunks
1 cup mayonnaise
½ cup **HOLLAND HOUSE® White Cooking Wine**
1 cup diced pecans or walnuts

Toss fruit, vegetables and cheese together in a large bowl. In a separate bowl, mix mayonnaise and wine. Add to fruit mixture, blending thoroughly. Chill. Garnish with pecans.   *Serves 6*

**Libby's
Libby's
Libby's**

Speedy Salad Suggestions

Top peach slices with cranberry-orange relish or pecan-stuffed dates. Serve on greens with an easy fruit dressing: Blend a small amount of grated orange rind and juice from **LIBBY'S® Juice Pack Peaches** into mayonnaise to make a pouring consistency.

Blend cream cheese with just enough juice from **LIBBY'S® Juice Pack Fruit Cocktail** to make it light and fluffy. Spoon over fruit on bed of greens; sprinkle with chopped walnuts.

San Giorgio®
Fruit and Shells Refresher

1 cup **SAN GIORGIO® Shell Macaroni**, uncooked
1 cup grape halves, seeded
1 cup (11-ounce can) mandarin oranges, drained
½ cup sliced celery
¾ cup (8-ounce can) pineapple chunks, undrained
1 cup vanilla yogurt
1 tablespoon honey
½ cup broken walnuts

Cook Shell Macaroni according to package directions; drain well. Cool. (Rinse with cold water to cool quickly; drain well.) Combine grapes, oranges and celery in medium bowl. Drain pineapple chunks, reserving 2 tablespoons juice; add pineapple chunks to fruit mixture. Combine yogurt, honey and reserved pineapple juice in small bowl; blend well. Pour dressing over fruit; toss. Add cooled Shell Macaroni; mix well. Chill; stir in walnuts just before serving. *6 to 8 servings*

Exotic Fruit Salad

Coarsely grate some rind from 1 or 2 oranges; set aside. Pare oranges, discarding remaining rind. Slice oranges, then cut slices into halves. Toss gently with sliced bananas and pears, toasted **BLUE RIBBON® Slivered Almonds** and a little chopped semisweet chocolate. For each serving, place a crisp lettuce cup on a chilled salad plate; fill, mounding, with the fruit mixture. Dollop generously with a dressing made with dairy sour cream or imitation, a splash of sherry, a dash of salt and the reserved orange rind, all briskly stirred together with a fork. Sprinkle a little more chopped chocolate over dressing.

Brandied Fruit Salad

1 cup (12 oz. can) pineapple chunks
1 cup halved fresh strawberries
½ cup California Brandy
1 (3 oz.) package lemon flavor gelatin
1 (3 oz.) package raspberry flavor gelatin
2 cups boiling water
3 tablespoons lemon juice
1 medium banana, sliced
½ cup sliced celery
2 tablespoons finely chopped preserved ginger
Lettuce
Sliced kiwi fruit
Whole strawberries

Drain pineapple thoroughly. Combine with halved strawberries and brandy, and let stand 20 minutes. Meanwhile, dissolve flavored gelatins in boiling water. Stir in lemon juice, and cool to room temperature. Add marinated fruits and brandy, and chill until slightly thickened. Add banana, celery and ginger. Turn into oiled 6-cup mold, and chill firm, at least 3 hours, (overnight for tall mold). At serving time, unmold, and garnish with lettuce, sliced kiwi and whole strawberries.

Makes 1 large salad, 6 to 8 servings

Favorite recipe from the **California Brandy Advisory Board**

Wheat Germ Fruit Salad

2 cups creamed cottage cheese
½ cup **KRETSCHMER Wheat Germ With Brown Sugar & Honey**
¼ cup raisins *or* diced dates
¼ cup chopped walnuts
2 tsp. vanilla
2 tsp. sugar
2 apples, sliced
Lettuce leaves

Combine all ingredients *except* apples and lettuce. Mix well. Arrange apple slices in fan shape on lettuce leaves. Top with cheese mixture. *Makes 4 servings*

Festive Fruit Salad

1 cup dairy sour cream
2 Tbsp. brown sugar
Grated peel of 1 **SUNKIST® Tangerine**
3 to 4 **SUNKIST® Tangerines**, peeled, segmented, seeded (about 2 cups)
1 apple, unpeeled, cubed
1 pear, unpeeled, cubed
1 banana, sliced
1 cup seedless grapes
½ cup coarsely chopped nuts

In large bowl, combine sour cream, brown sugar and tangerine peel. Stir in remaining ingredients; chill. Serve on salad greens, if desired. *Makes 6 servings (about 5½ cups)*

Fresh Fruit Salad

8 cups of cut-up mixed fresh fruit such as: oranges, apples, bananas, pears, peaches, strawberries, grapes
Bibb lettuce

Line a large salad bowl with Bibb lettuce leaves. Fill salad bowl with fruit. Accompany with Poppy Seed Fruit Salad Dressing* *6 to 8 servings*

*Poppy Seed Fruit Salad Dressing

¾ cup sugar
1½ teaspoons onion salt
1 teaspoon dry mustard
⅓ cup vinegar
1 cup **CRISCO® Oil**
1 tablespoon poppy seed

In a small bowl combine sugar, salt, and dry mustard. Stir in vinegar. Beat at medium speed while gradually adding **CRISCO® Oil**. Beat 5 to 10 minutes longer, until thickened. Add poppy seeds. Pour into a screw-top jar. Cover tightly and shake vigorously to blend well. Store covered in refrigerator. Shake well before using. Serve on fresh fruit salads, grapefruit sections, or on lettuce wedges. *About 1⅔ cup*

Lemon Whipped Fruit Salad

2 quarts water
2 teaspoons salt
1 tablespoon oil
1½ cups AMERICAN BEAUTY® SALAD-RONI® or 1¾ cups ELBO-RONI®
4-oz. pkg. lemon-flavored instant pudding and pie filling
1½-oz. envelope whipped topping mix
2 cups milk
2 (13-oz.) cans fruit cocktail, drained
1 cup diced apple
½ cup chopped nuts
1½ teaspoons grated lemon rind, if desired

Boil water in large deep pot with salt and oil (to prevent boiling over). Add SALAD-RONI®; stir to separate. Cook uncovered after water returns to a full rolling boil for 8 to 9 minutes. Stir occasionally. Drain and rinse under cold water.

In medium bowl, combine dry pudding, whipped topping mix and milk. Beat at high speed until light and fluffy, about 2 minutes. In large bowl, combine remaining ingredients; fold in pudding mixture. Refrigerate at least 1 hour to blend flavors.

16 (½-cup) servings

High Altitude—Above 3500 Feet: Cooking times may need to be increased slightly for SALAD-RONI®; no additional changes.

NUTRITION INFORMATION PER SERVING
SERVING SIZE: 1/16 of recipe

		PERCENT U.S. RDA	
Calories	155	PER SERVING	
Protein	4g	Protein	6
Carbohydrate	26g	Vitamin A	2
Fat	5g	Vitamin C	3
Sodium	67mg	Thiamine	6
Potassium	170mg	Riboflavin	5
		Niacin	4
		Calcium	5
		Iron	5

PET®

Overnight Fruit Salad

1½ cups miniature marshmallows
1 can (20 oz.) pineapple chunks, drained
1 can (11 oz.) mandarin oranges, drained
1 cup shredded coconut
1 can (8 oz.) PET® Imitation Sour Cream

Toss all ingredients together. Refrigerate overnight for best flavor. Serve on lettuce as a salad or top with melted orange marmalade for a dessert. *Makes 9 servings, ½ cup each*

Deviled Smithfield Ham and Cream Cheese on Pineapple Salad

Place a round of pineapple on crisp lettuce. Mix teaspoonful of AMBER BRAND Deviled SMITHFIELD Ham and teaspoon of cream cheese. Fill center of pineapple-round with the mixture.

THE CHRISTIAN BROTHERS®

Melon Mosaic

1 small watermelon
1 small cantaloupe
1 small honeydew melon
1 cup blueberries, raspberries or grapes
⅔ cup sugar
1 cup THE CHRISTIAN BROTHERS® Chateau La Salle Light Wine
1 lime

With sharp knife, cut watermelon into scalloped basket. With a melon scooper, form melons into balls. Combine sugar and wine in small saucepan; heat to boiling. Add 1 tsp. grated lime rind and squeezed lime juice; cool. Pour over melon balls and blueberries. Chill, covered, several hours. Serve in watermelon basket. Garnish with mint, if desired. *Serves 8*

Fruit Salad With Tangy Cheese Dressing

Fruit:
Lettuce Leaves
1 (20-ounce) can pineapple slices in natural juices, reserving ¼ cup juice
1 (8¼-ounce) can pineapple slices in natural juices, drained
1 (16-ounce) can pear halves, drained
1 (16-ounce) can peach slices, drained
¾ pound red grapes

Dressing:
⅓ cup dairy sour cream
¼ cup SNACK MATE Sharp Cheddar Pasteurized Process Cheese Spread
¼ cup reserved pineapple juice
1 tablespoon lemon juice

Garnish:
2 tablespoons toasted slivered almonds or
1 tablespoon toasted sesame seeds

1. **Make Salad:** Cover individual salad plates or large serving platter with lettuce leaves. Arrange pineapple slices, pear halves, peach slices and grapes attractively on lettuce. Cover and chill.
2. **Make Dressing:** In medium bowl, using electric mixer at medium speed, beat together sour cream, SNACK MATE Cheese, pineapple juice and lemon juice. Cover and chill.
3. **To Serve:** Pour dressing over salad and sprinkle with toasted almonds or sesame seeds; or pass dressing separately.

Makes 6 servings

Tropicana Salad

1 well-chilled cantaloupe, peeled and diced
2 large bananas, sliced
1 or more kiwi fruits, sliced
1 cup miniature marshmallows
½ cup pecan halves
½ cup mayonnaise
1½ oz. HIRAM WALKER Creme de Banana

Combine prepared fruit with marshmallows and pecans. Blend mayonnaise and Creme de Banana together and gently mix with fruit combination. Chill. Serve on salad greens. *Serves 4 to 6*

Fruit in the Sun at Midnight

4 medium size ripe cantaloupes
1 pint raspberries
1 pint blueberries
½ pound green grapes, halved
½ cup kirschwasser or sauterne
1 package (6 ounces) **VALIO Gruyere Cheese**
Fresh mint sprigs

Using pencil, mark a line completely around outside of cantaloupe. Cut in half carefully being sure to cut through to center. Remove seeds. Scoop out melon in balls, leaving ½-inch shell. Refrigerate shells. Combine fruits and liquor. Refrigerate at least 1 hour. Meanwhile, cut cheese into strips or small cubes. Just before serving, combine cheese and marinated fruit. Spoon into cantaloupe shells. Garnish with mint.   *Makes 8 servings*

Banana-Nut Salad

1 tablespoon **JIF® Creamy Peanut Butter**
1 tablespoon honey
¼ cup mayonnaise or salad dressing
Bananas
Lemon juice
Shredded lettuce
Chopped peanuts

In small bowl, stir together the **JIF®** and honey. Blend in mayonnaise or salad dressing. Cut bananas in half lengthwise; dip in lemon juice. Arrange banana halves on shredded lettuce in salad dishes. Spread **JIF®** mixture on bananas; sprinkle with nuts.

Quick Applesauce-Cottage Cheese Salad

2 cups thick applesauce (1 #303 can)
1 cup cottage cheese
1 pkg. lime gelatin
¾ cup boiling water

Combine applesauce and cottage cheese. Dissolve lime gelatin in boiling water and then fold into applesauce-cottage cheese mixture. Pour into 8-inch square pan. Refrigerate.

Favorite recipe from the **Michigan Apple Committee**

Kiwi in Pineapple Shell

1 large pineapple
1½ cups strawberries, quartered lengthwise
4 kiwifruit, peeled
⅓ cup sliced, toasted almonds
¼ cup shredded coconut
½ cup **GIBSON Kiwifruit Wine**
2 tablespoons dry vermouth
Sprigs of mint

Slice pineapple in half lengthwise, through crown. Use knife to cut fruit away from both half shells. Trim away core; cut pineapple and 1 kiwifruit into chunks. Combine with remaining ingredients and set aside. Slice remaining 3 kiwifruit and place around edges of shells. Fill shells with fruit mixture. Garnish with mint. Serve chilled.   *6-8 servings*

Sun World® Summer Salad

5 Tbsp. honey
Juice of 1 lemon
½ cup water
2 cantaloupes
2 oranges, peeled and cut into segments
½ honeydew melon
8 **SUN WORLD® Dates**, pitted and quartered
1 dessert apple, cored and diced in large pieces
1 cup black grapes, halved and seeded

Mix the honey, lemon juice and water and boil for 2 minutes. Halve the melons, remove the seeds and scoop out the flesh with a ball scoop. Mix with the other fruits. Pour the cooled honey syrup over the fruit salad and pile into the 4 cantaloupe shells.

Emerald Salad With Yogurt Dressing

3 **CAPE GRANNY SMITH Apples**, cored and cubed
  (about 4 cups)
2 cups honeydew melon balls
2 cups green grapes, halved
2 kiwi fruit, pared and thinly sliced
¼ cup orange juice

In large bowl combine all ingredients; mix well. Cover. Chill. Serve with Yogurt Dressing.*   *Yield: 8 servings*

*Yogurt Dressing

2 containers (8 ounces each) plain yogurt
3 tablespoons confectioners' sugar
2 tablespoons orange juice
½ teaspoon grated orange peel
¼ teaspoon ground cinnamon
⅛ teaspoon ground mace

In a bowl, combine all ingredients; mix well. Spoon over fruit salad.

Favorite recipe from the **Cape Granny Smith Apples**

Layered Fruit Salad

2 cups (16 oz.) **BREAKSTONE'S® Smooth and Creamy Style Cottage Cheese**
1 8¼ oz. can crushed pineapple, drained
½ cup toasted coconut
2 cups banana chunks
2 cups red grape halves, seeded
2 cups nectarine or peach slices
2 cups pear slices
1 cup strawberry halves

Combine cottage cheese, pineapple and coconut; mix well. In 2-quart bowl, layer bananas, grapes, half of cottage cheese mixture, nectarines, pears and remaining cottage cheese mixture. Top with strawberries.   *6 to 8 servings*

Kellogg's®

Lemony Apple-Bran Salad

½ cup lemon yogurt
1 tablespoon finely snipped fresh parsley
2 cups cubed, unpared red apples (about ½ lb., 1 to 2 medium-size)
½ cup thinly sliced celery
½ cup halved red grapes
½ cup **KELLOGG'S® ALL-BRAN®** or **KELLOGG'S® BRAN BUDS®** Cereal
6 lettuce leaves

Stir together yogurt, parsley, apples, celery and grapes. Cover and chill thoroughly. At serving time, stir in **KELLOGG'S® ALL-BRAN®** Cereal. Serve on lettuce leaves.

Yield: 6 servings

® Kellogg Company

Half-Moon Honeydew Boats

(Low Calorie)

1 honeydew melon, halved and seeded
1 pkg. (43 grams) **ESTEE® Strawberry Gel**
½ cup fresh or frozen sliced strawberries, unsweetened
½ medium banana, peeled & sliced

Prepare **ESTEE® Strawberry Gel** as directed on package. Cool 5 minutes. Gently stir in strawberry and banana slices. Fill melon halves with gel mixture. Refrigerate until set. To serve, cut each melon half into 3 slices.

Makes 6 servings, ⅙ melon per serving

NUTRITION INFORMATION

Calories	Carbohydrates	Protein	Sodium
89	21g	1g	22mg

DIABETIC EXCHANGE INFORMATION

Fruit
2

Two Fingers® Fruit Salad

1 small fresh pineapple
2 navel oranges
6 kiwi fruit
3 medium-size bananas
3 cups halved strawberries
Lettuce
TWO FINGERS® Creamy Fruit Dressing*

With large heavy knife, peel pineapple; remove eyes with small knife, and cut pineapple into chunks, removing core (should measure about 3 cups). Peel kiwis, and slice crosswise. Peel and slice bananas. Peel and break oranges into sections. Arrange fruits in groups on lettuce-garnished plate. Pass Creamy Fruit Dressing.

Makes 6 servings (about 1½ cups each)

• Substitute any fresh, in-season fruits for those suggested, keeping an eye on color, texture and flavor variety. *(Continued)*

*Two Fingers® Creamy Fruit Dressing

¼ cup sugar
1½ tablespoons flour
¾ teaspoon dry mustard
¼ teaspoon salt
¾ cup orange juice
¼ cup **TWO FINGERS® Tequila**
1 tablespoon lime juice
1 large egg, beaten
½ cup plain yogurt

Mix sugar, flour, mustard and salt together well in 1-quart saucepan. Gradually stir in orange juice, mixing until smooth. Add tequila and lime juice. Stir over moderate heat until mixture comes to a boil. Cook for 1 minute, stirring constantly, until mixture is thickened. Stir a little of the hot mixture into beaten egg. Combine with remaining mixture, and cook about 30 seconds longer over very low heat, stirring briskly. Remove from heat; cool. When cold, stir in yogurt. *Makes 1½ cups dressing*

• Serve poured over individual fruit salads, or as a dip for individual fruit pieces.

THE ORIGINAL WORCESTERSHIRE

Fruit Bowl Salad*

2 red apples, cored and diced
1 pear, peeled, cored and diced
1 banana, peeled and sliced
1 cup diced celery
½ cup coarsely chopped walnuts
½ cup mayonnaise
2 tablespoons lemon juice
1½ teaspoons sugar
1½ teaspoons **LEA & PERRINS Worcestershire Sauce**

In a salad bowl combine apples, pear, banana, celery and walnuts. Mix remaining ingredients. Pour over salad; toss gently. Serve on lettuce-lined salad bowl, if desired. *Yield: 6 portions*

*May be prepared in advance of serving.

Peanut-Dressed Melon Salad

1 7-ounce jar (2 cups) marshmallow creme
½ cup unsweetened pineapple juice
½ cup **JIF® Creamy Peanut Butter**
2 tablespoons lemon juice
Dash salt
1 cup cantaloupe balls
1 cup watermelon pieces
1 cup sliced peaches
1 cup seedless green grapes

In blender container, combine first 5 ingredients. Cover and blend smooth. Chill. Arrange fruit on lettuce-lined plate. Serve with **JIF®** mixture.

Boggs® Orange Salad

½ cup **BOGGS® Cranberry Liqueur**
¼ cup oil
½ teaspoon sugar
2 teaspoons lemon juice
2 teaspoons **GREY POUPON® Dijon Mustard**
3 oranges, peeled, thinly sliced
1 banana, peeled, thinly sliced
Boston or Bibb lettuce
Toasted sesame seeds

In small bowl, combine **BOGGS®**, oil, sugar, lemon juice and mustard. Arrange oranges and bananas on bed of lettuce. Spoon dressing over fruit. Sprinkle with sesame seeds. *Serves 6*

Featherweight®

Grapefruit/Almond Salad

(Low Calorie/Low Sodium)

1 can (16 oz.) **FEATHERWEIGHT® Grapefruit Segments**, drained
¼ cup blanched almonds, sliced
¼ cup dates, chopped
1 green pepper, cut into rings

Sweeten to taste with **FEATHERWEIGHT® Sweetening**. **FEATHERWEIGHT® Salad Dressing** (optional). Toss all together and chill. *Serves 4-5*

Approx.	Calories	Protein (Grams)	Fat (Grams)	Carbohydrate (Grams)	Sodium (Mgs.)
½ cup serving	75	1	2	7	4

Milnot® Frozen Fruit Salad

1 can (16 oz.) fruit cocktail
1 package (3 oz.) cream cheese, softened
1 tablespoon lemon juice
¼ cup sugar
⅛ teaspoon salt
6 marshmallows, quartered
⅓ cup **MILNOT®**, whipped

Drain fruit cocktail reserving 2 tablespoons of syrup. Mix cheese, lemon juice, sugar, salt, and reserved syrup until smooth. Add marshmallows; fold into fruit cocktail. Fold whipped **MILNOT®** into fruit mixture. Pour into ice cube tray (or loaf pan) and freeze until firm. (No stirring needed). *Yield: approx. 1 quart*

Frozen Fruit Salad

1 package (3¾ ounces) instant vanilla pudding mix
1 cup mayonnaise
½ cup milk
2½ tablespoons lemon juice
1 can (30 ounces) fruit cocktail, drained
1 medium banana, peeled, sliced
2 cups **FIRESIDE Miniature Marshmallows**
1 cup whipping cream, whipped
⅓ cup coarsely chopped pecans

Beat pudding mix, mayonnaise, milk and lemon juice until smooth and thickened. Fold in remaining ingredients. Spoon into 13 x 9 x 2-inch pan. Cover; freeze. Let stand at room temperature 15 minutes before serving. *12 servings*

Solo® Frozen Fruit Salad

1-8 oz. package cream cheese, softened
½ tsp. salt
1 cup mayonnaise
3 Tbsp. lemon juice
1 jar (16 oz.) **SOLO® Strawberry Glaze** or pkg. **SOLO® Strawberry Glaze Dry Mix**
1 can (15 oz.) crushed pineapple, drained
2 bananas, sliced
½ cup chopped nuts
1 cup whipping cream
¼ cup sugar

Mix cream cheese, salt, mayonnaise, lemon juice and **SOLO® Glaze** until well blended. Add pineapple, bananas and nuts. Whip cream until thick, adding sugar 1 tablespoon at a time. Combine whipped cream and cream cheese mixture. Pour into 9″ × 13″ pan and freeze until firm. *Serves 16*

Gelatin Salads

KNOX®

Fresh Asparagus Chicken Salad

3 envelopes **KNOX® Unflavored Gelatine**
4 cups chicken broth, divided
12 fresh asparagus spears (about 1 pound)
4 to 5 fresh mushrooms thinly sliced
3 cups cooked chicken, chopped
1½ cups chopped celery
¼ cup chopped onion
½ cup bottled Italian dressing
2 tablespoons fresh lemon juice
Salad greens
Lemon slices

In medium bowl, mix unflavored gelatine with 1½ cups cold chicken broth. Heat remaining 2½ cups broth to boiling; add to gelatine mixture and stir until gelatine is completely dissolved. Chill until mixture is the consistency of unbeaten egg whites. Meanwhile, cut asparagus spears into 8-inch lengths; wash and trim. Cook asparagus in 1-inch boiling salted water in covered skillet, 8 minutes or until crisp-tender. Arrange asparagus and mushrooms on bottom of 8 x 12 x 2-inch (2-quart) baking dish. Pour 2 cups gelatine mixture over vegetables; chill until almost set. Combine chicken, celery, onion, Italian dressing and lemon juice; mix well. Spread chicken salad over gelatine. Pour remaining 2 cups gelatine over chicken salad. Refrigerate at least 4 hours, or overnight. Unmold onto serving plate. Garnish with salad greens and lemon slices. *Makes 6 servings*

Apple Sauce Ham Salad

2 envelopes plain gelatin
½ cup cold **LUCKY LEAF®** Apple Juice
1 cup hot **LUCKY LEAF®** Apple Juice
¼ tsp. salt
1 Tbsp. white **LUCKY LEAF®** Vinegar
3 Tbsp. diced pimiento
2 cups **LUCKY LEAF®** Apple Sauce
1 cup diced celery
1 cup shredded carrots
2 Tbsp. grated onion
1½ cups cubed cooked ham
3 Tbsp. diced green pepper

Soften gelatin in cold apple juice. Add to hot apple juice and stir to dissolve. Add salt, vinegar, pimiento and apple sauce. Chill. When mixture begins to thicken, add remaining ingredients. Pour into a pan (11″ × 7″) that has been rinsed in cold water, or pour into individual molds. Chill until firm. *Serves eight*

Gelatin Shrimp Mold

1½ cups **THANK YOU®** Brand Tomato Juice
1 3 oz. package Lemon Gelatin
2 8 oz. packages Cream Cheese, softened
1 cup Mayonnaise
2 tablespoons Chopped Onion
2 cups finely Chopped Celery
½ cup chopped Green Pepper
½ cup sliced Pimiento Stuffed Green Olives
1 6½ oz. can of Shrimp drained

Heat tomato juice, add gelatin to dissolve. Cool, add cream cheese and blend well. Add mayonnaise and continue to blend. Electric mixer may be used if desired. Fold in remaining ingredients. Mix well. Pour into a mold and refrigerate until set. Unmold and serve with crackers.

Vegetable Seafood Aspic

2 pkgs. unflavored gelatin
4 cups **S&W® "Spring"** Vegetable Juice Cocktail
1 tsp. Worcestershire sauce
2-3 drops hot pepper sauce
½ cup finely chopped celery
¼ cup finely chopped green onion
¼ cup sliced black olives
1-6½ oz. can chunk light tuna, drained well
Sliced black olives and sour cream as desired for garnish

Dissolve gelatin in ½ cup vegetable juice cocktail. Heat the remaining 3½ cups vegetable juice cocktail, and combine gelatin mixture, Worcestershire sauce and hot pepper sauce with it. Blend well and refrigerate until partially set. Fold in remaining ingredients and pour into a 6 to 8 cup mold. Chill until firm. Unmold onto a bed of red leaf lettuce and decorate with sliced black olives and a dollop of sour cream. Serve with crusty French rolls, a wedge of cheese and iced tea. *Serves 4-6*

Smithfield Ham Aspic Salad

16 cups hot water
1 cup unflavored gelatin
3 cups **AMBER BRAND Deviled SMITHFIELD Ham**
1 cup chili sauce
12 hard-boiled eggs

Dissolve gelatin in hot water, stir in the **AMBER BRAND Ham**, chili sauce and pour into cup molds. Cut eggs in half, dividing the yolks; sink the divided egg-halves in the gelatin solution—when it is about set. Chill thoroughly, remove from molds, serve on lettuce with mayonnaise. *Serves 24*

Aspic Ring à la Mr. and Mrs. "T"®

2 cups or cans **MR. & MRS. "T"®** Bloody Mary Mix
1 cup or can **MR. & MRS. "T"®** Bully-Hi Mix
3 envelopes unflavored gelatin
1 small package cooked shrimp
1 avocado
⅓ cup chopped celery
⅓ cup chopped cucumber
⅓ cup chopped onion

Heat **MR. & MRS. "T"® Bloody Mary Mix, Bully-Hi Mix** and gelatin to boiling point. *Do not boil.* Cool to room temperature. Paint sides of 3½ cup mold with gelatin mixture. Place shrimp and avocado fancifully about the mold. Place mold in freezer for a few minutes to set. Meanwhile, add chopped celery, cucumber and onion to the remainder of the gelatin mixture. Pour into the mold. Chill in refrigerator for about 2 hours. *Serves 4*

Garden Fresh Salad
(Low Calorie/Low Fat)

1 envelope unflavored gelatin
¾ cup water
1 cup tomato juice
2 tablespoons vinegar
Dash hot pepper sauce
2 packets **SWEET 'N LOW®**
1 cup chopped celery, cucumber, or green pepper
2 tablespoons chopped red onion

In medium saucepan, soften gelatin in water. Heat and stir until gelatin is completely dissolved. Stir in tomato juice, vinegar, hot pepper sauce, and **SWEET 'N LOW®**. Chill, stirring occasionally, about 1 hour, or until mixture is consistency of unbeaten egg whites. Fold in vegetables. Turn into 3-cup mold or bowl and chill until firm. *6 servings*

Per Serving (½ cup): Calories: 20; Fat: trace

Lemony Snow

½ cup **KOOL-AID® Sugar-Sweetened Lemonade Mix**
⅓ cup sugar
1 envelope unflavored gelatin
¼ teaspoon salt
1¼ cups boiling water
2 egg whites

Combine soft drink mix, sugar, gelatin and salt in a bowl. Add boiling water and stir until gelatin is dissolved. Chill until thickened. Add egg whites and beat with electric mixer until fluffy and thick and double in volume. Pour into a 3- or 4-cup mold, individual molds, individual dessert glasses or a serving bowl. Chill until firm, about 2 hours. Unmold. Serve with custard sauce, or sweetened fruit and garnish with whole fresh strawberries, if desired.

Makes 3 cups or 6 servings

Fresh 'n Natural Gazpacho Salad

3 envelopes **KNOX® Unflavored Gelatine**
1½ cups beef broth
¼ cup wine vinegar
2 tablespoons fresh lemon juice
2 teaspoons Worcestershire sauce
1 teaspoon salt
⅛ teaspoon hot pepper sauce
3 cups chopped fresh tomatoes
1 cup finely chopped green pepper
½ cup finely chopped celery
¼ cup finely chopped onion
1 clove garlic, minced

In medium saucepan, mix unflavored gelatine with cold broth; let stand 1 minute. Stir over medium heat until gelatine is completely dissolved, about 2 minutes. Remove from heat; stir in vinegar, lemon juice, Worcestershire sauce, salt and hot pepper sauce. Chill, until mixture is the consistency of unbeaten egg whites. Fold in remaining ingredients. Turn into individual cups or molds or a 6-cup ring mold. Chill until firm. Unmold on lettuce leaves, if desired.

Makes 8 servings

Royal Pear Salad

1 cup boiling water
1 package (6 ounces) raspberry-flavored gelatin
2 cups cold water
1 can (16 ounces) whole cranberry sauce
1 can (29 ounces) **STOKELY'S FINEST® Bartlett Pear Halves**, drained
½ cup chopped walnuts
½ teaspoon lemon juice

Stir gelatin into boiling water until dissolved. Add cold water and cranberry sauce. Stir to blend. Chill until almost set. Cut all but 3 pear halves into chunks; slice reserved pear halves and set aside. Stir pear chunks, nuts, and lemon juice into gelatin mixture. Pour into 6-cup mold. Chill at least 6 hours, or until firm. Unmold on bed of lettuce, garnish with sliced pears, and serve.

7 to 8 servings

Scarlett O'Hara Salad

1¼ cups **OCEAN SPRAY Cranberry Juice Cocktail**
1 3 oz. pkg. cherry gelatin
½ cup **SOUTHERN COMFORT®**
3 Tbsp. lime or lemon juice
½ cup sugar
1 cup seedless grapes, halved
½ cup finely chopped celery
1 cup pitted canned Bing cherries
½ cup chopped walnuts or pecans

Heat cranberry juice; stir in gelatin till dissolved. Remove from heat. Add **SOUTHERN COMFORT®**, lime or lemon juice, and sugar. Chill until mixture begins to congeal. Fold in remaining ingredients. Chill until firm in lightly oiled mold. Unmold on lettuce.

Serves 10

Zesty Cranberry-Nut Mold

(Low Calorie/Low Fat)

1 pkg. (47 grams) **ESTEE® Orange Gel**
1½ cups low calorie cranberry juice
½ cup low calorie ginger ale
1 orange, peeled, seeded and chopped
¼ cup walnuts, chopped

Mix cranberry juice and ginger ale in saucepan and heat to a boil. Empty **ESTEE® Orange Gel** into medium bowl. Pour hot liquid over gel and stir until dissolved. Cool 5 minutes. Gently stir in orange and walnut pieces. Pour into 3-cup mold. Refrigerate until set.

Makes 6 servings, ½ cup per serving

NUTRITION INFORMATION

Calories	Carbohydrates	Protein	Fat
76	11g	1g	3g

DIABETIC EXCHANGE INFORMATION

Fruit	Fat
1	½

Peach Sauterne Salad

1 can (17 oz.) sliced peaches
2 packages (3 oz. each) or 1 package (6 oz.) **JELL-O® Peach Flavor Gelatin**
1½ cups sauterne wine
2 teaspoons lemon juice
1 medium apple, diced

Drain peaches, reserving syrup. Dice the peaches. Add water to syrup to make 2 cups; bring to a boil. Dissolve gelatin in boiling liquid. Stir in wine and lemon juice and chill until thickened. Fold in peaches and apple. Spoon into 5-cup mold. Chill until firm, about 4 hours. Unmold. Garnish with salad greens, if desired.

Makes 5 cups or 10 servings

Jellied Angostura® Salad

1 package lemon-flavored gelatin
1 cup tomato juice
1 tablespoon ANGOSTURA® bitters
½ teaspoon salt
1 cup grated carrot

Make gelatin as directed on package, substituting tomato juice for 1 cup of cold water. Add ANGOSTURA® and salt. Chill until it begins to thicken, then add the grated carrot. Mix well and place in salad mold. Chill until firm. *Yield: 6 servings*

Gerber.
Rainbow Gelatin

1 package (3 oz.) cherry gelatin
1 jar (4½ oz.) GERBER® Strained Beets
1 package (3 oz.) lime gelatin
1 jar (4½ oz.) GERBER® Strained Peas
1 package (3 oz.) lemon gelatin
1 jar (4½ oz.) GERBER® Strained Creamed Corn
1 package (3 oz.) orange gelatin
1 jar (4¾ oz.) GERBER® Strained Sweet Potatoes

Dissolve cherry gelatin in 1½ cups boiling water. Add beets and chill in a 9 × 13 inch pan until set. While first layer is chilling, dissolve lime gelatin in 1½ cups boiling water, add peas and cool. When first layer is set, pour cooled lime gelatin mixture over first layer and chill until set. Repeat this procedure with lemon gelatin dissolved in 1½ cups boiling water and corn; orange gelatin dissolved in 1½ cups boiling water and sweet potatoes, until all layers are set. When completely set, cut in squares and serve. *Yield: 16-20 servings*

Southern Belle Salad

1 can (16 oz.) pitted dark sweet cherries
1 pkg. (3 oz.) cherry gelatin
1 cup COCA-COLA®
2 tablespoons fresh lemon juice
1 pkg. (3 oz.) cream cheese
½ cup cut-up pecans or walnuts

Drain cherry juice. Bring ¾ cup of the juice to boiling; add to gelatin. Stir until dissolved. Stir in COCA-COLA® and lemon juice. Chill until gelatin mounds slightly. Cut cheese into very small pieces. Fold cheese, nuts and whole cherries into gelatin. Spoon into 7 individual molds. Chill until firm. *Makes 7 (½ cup) servings*

KNOX.
California Fruit Salad Rosé

1 envelope KNOX® Unflavored Gelatine
2 tablespoons sugar
¾ cup boiling water
1¼ cups rosé wine
1 cup thinly sliced peaches
½ cup sliced banana
½ cup sliced strawberries

In medium bowl, mix unflavored gelatine with sugar; add boiling water and stir until gelatine is completely dissolved. Stir in wine. Chill, stirring occasionally, until mixture is consistency of unbeaten egg whites. Fold in peaches, banana and strawberries. Turn into 4-cup mold or bowl and chill until firm. *Makes about 6 servings*

Cranberry Orchard Salad

1½ cups ground fresh cranberries
½ cup sugar
2 packages (3 oz. each) or 1 package (6 oz.) JELL-O® Orange or Lemon Flavor Gelatin
¼ teaspoon salt
2 cups boiling water
1½ cups cold water
1 tablespoon lemon juice
¼ teaspoon cinnamon
⅛ teaspoon cloves
1 orange, sectioned and diced
½ cup chopped walnuts or almonds*

Combine cranberries and sugar and set aside. Dissolve gelatin and salt in boiling water. Add cold water, lemon juice, cinnamon and cloves. Chill until thickened. Fold in the cranberries, orange and nuts. Spoon into 6-cup mold. Chill until firm, about 4 hours. Unmold. Garnish with salad greens, if desired. *Makes about 6 cups or 12 servings*

*Or use ½ cup chopped celery.

Apple Bits Mold

1 envelope unflavored gelatin
½ cup cold water
1 (12 oz.) can DIET SHASTA® Strawberry
¼ teaspoon salt
⅛ teaspoon cinnamon
⅛ teaspoon nutmeg
1 tablespoon lemon juice
¼ teaspoon artificial liquid sweetener
1 cup diced apple

Soften gelatin in water. Stir over hot water until dissolved. Add all remaining ingredients, except apple. Chill until mixture begins to thicken. Fold in apples. Spoon into individual molds or small ring mold and chill until firm. *Makes about 2½ cups (4 servings)*

Molded Fruit Salad

1 3-oz. package fruit-flavored gelatin
2 cups hot water
½ cup MARSHMALLOW FLUFF®
1½ cups drained diced mixed fruit

Dissolve gelatin in hot water; stir in FLUFF®. Mix thoroughly, then chill until thickened and mounds when dropped from a spoon. Fold in fruit and turn into individual molds or custard cups. Chill until firm. *Makes 6 servings*

Frosty Green Sour Cream Mold

2 3 oz. packages lime flavored gelatin
2 cups boiling water
1 20½ oz. can, crushed pineapple, drained
½ pint (1 cup) sour cream
⅓ cup chopped pecans
1 8 oz. package **BORDO Imported Diced Dates**

Mix gelatin and water until gelatin is dissolved. Chill until thick, but not completely set. Whip with electric mixer or hand beater until frothy and light. Add sour cream and mix well. Fold in drained crushed pineapple, pecans and dates. Pour into lightly greased 6 cup mold. Chill until firm. *Serves 8-10*

Ruby Borscht Salad

1 can (1 lb., 4 oz.) **DOLE® Crushed Pineapple**
1 package (6 oz.) wild raspberry gelatin
1½ cups boiling water
1 can (1 lb.) shoestring beets
3 tablespoons plain vinegar
1 teaspoon dill weed
Dash salt
1 cup chopped celery
Dairy sour cream

Drain pineapple reserving all syrup. Dissolve gelatin in boiling water. Stir in beets and all liquid, vinegar, dill, salt and reserved pineapple syrup. Chill until mixture thickens to consistency of unbeaten egg white. Fold in celery and pineapple. Pour into 2-quart mold. Chill firm. Top with sour cream and a sprinkle of dill weed to serve. *Makes 8 servings*

Molded Pineapple-Orange Salad

1 package (6 oz.) orange flavored gelatin
2 cups boiling water
1 cup cold water
1 can (15¼ oz.) pineapple chunks, drained (reserve ½ cup pineapple juice)
½ cup prepared **HIDDEN VALLEY ORIGINAL RANCH® Salad Dressing**
1 cup finely chopped celery
1 can (11 oz.) mandarin orange segments, drained
½ cup finely chopped walnuts

Dissolve gelatin in boiling water. Add cold water and reserved pineapple juice. Chill until syrupy. Mix in remaining ingredients. Spoon into ungreased 2 quart mold. Chill until firm.

Makes 8 to 10 servings

JELL-O® GELATIN DESSERT
Muffin Pan Fruit Salad

1 package (3 oz.) **JELL-O® Orange Flavor Gelatin Dessert**
⅛ teaspoon salt
⅛ teaspoon ginger
1½ cups boiling water
2 teaspoons lemon juice
1½ cups (about) fruit combination*

Dissolve gelatin, salt and ginger in boiling water. Add lemon juice. Place aluminum foil cupcake liners in muffin pan. Place fruit combination in cups, filling each about ⅔ full. Then fill with gelatin mixture. Chill until firm, about 2 hours. Unmold carefully from foil cups. Serve with crisp salad greens, if desired.
Makes about 3 cups or 8 servings

*SUGGESTED FRUIT COMBINATIONS:

1 can (8¾ oz.) fruit cocktail, drained, and ½ cup diced celery
¾ cup *each* diced fresh peaches and orange sections
¾ cup *each* diced apple and pear
¾ cup *each* diced cantaloupe and honeydew melon

Muffin Pan Salad

1 package (3 oz.) **JELL-O® Lemon Flavor Gelatin Dessert**
½ teaspoon salt
¼ teaspoon celery salt
1½ cups boiling water
2 teaspoons vinegar
½ teaspoon prepared horseradish
1½ cups (about) fruit or vegetable combination*

Dissolve gelatin, salt and celery salt in boiling water. Add vinegar and horseradish. Place aluminum foil cupcake liners in muffin pan. Place salad ingredients in cups, filling each about ⅔ full. Then fill with gelatin mixture. Chill until firm, about 2 hours. Unmold carefully from foil cups. Serve with crisp salad greens, if desired. *Makes about 3 cups or 8 servings*

*SUGGESTED COMBINATIONS:

2 medium oranges, sectioned and diced and 1 small red onion, sliced into rings
1½ cups cooked mixed vegetables and 1 tablespoon grated onion
¾ cup *each* shredded zucchini and carrot and 2 tablespoons minced onion
1 cup cauliflower florets and ½ cup diced green pepper

Lindsay.
Lindsay® Olive-Nectar Salad

½ cup **LINDSAY® Pitted Ripe Olives**
1 (3 oz.) package lime-flavored gelatin
1½ cups pear nectar
½ cup diced cucumber
Crisp lettuce
Green mayonnaise

Cut olives into wedges. Heat nectar to almost boiling. Stir in gelatin until dissolved. Cool, then chill until mixture thickens. Fold in olive wedges and cucumber. Spoon into individual molds; chill until firm. Turn out on crisp lettuce. Serve with Green Mayonnaise made by adding 1 tablespoon each chopped green onion and parsley to ½ cup mayonnaise. Garnish with pitted ripe olives. *Serves 6*

Sunshine Citrus Mold

(Low Calorie/Low Fat/Low Sodium)

1 can (8 ounces) juice-packed crushed pineapple
2 cans (6½ ounces each) mandarin orange segments
2 envelopes unflavored gelatin
1 packet **SWEET 'N LOW®**
⅓ cup chopped walnuts
1 can (12 ounces) diet ginger ale, chilled

Drain fruit, reserving juice. In small saucepan, soften gelatin in juice, then heat and stir until gelatin is dissolved. Stir in **SWEET 'N LOW®**. Transfer to medium-size bowl and refrigerate about 45 minutes until chilled but not set. Stir in fruit and walnuts. Slowly pour ginger ale down side of bowl; stir gently until blended. Chill until partially set, about 45 minutes. Spoon into individual ½-cup molds. Chill till firm, about 1 hour. Unmold. *8 servings*

Per Serving (½ cup): Calories: 71; Fat: 3g; Sodium: 3mg

Salad Dressings

Creamy Blue Cheese Dressing

1 cup **BEST FOODS®/HELLMAN'S® Real Mayonnaise**
4 ounces blue cheese, crumbled
3 tablespoons milk
2 tablespoons lemon juice or dry white wine
1 tablespoon finely chopped onion
2 teaspoons sugar
¼ teaspoon salt
¼ teaspoon dry mustard
¼ teaspoon Worcestershire sauce

In small bowl stir together **Real Mayonnaise**, cheese, milk, lemon juice, onion, sugar, salt, mustard and Worcestershire sauce until well mixed. Cover; refrigerate at least 2 hours to blend flavors. *Makes about 1½ cups*

Roquefort Cream Dressing

2 tablespoons crumbled **ROQUEFORT Cheese**
½ cup sour cream
1 teaspoon vinegar
½ teaspoon salt
¼ teaspoon pepper
½ teaspoon chopped parsley
½ teaspoon dried tarragon
1 head iceberg lettuce, shredded

Place **ROQUEFORT Cheese** in a bowl. Gradually add sour cream, vinegar, salt, pepper, parsley and tarragon. Stir with a wooden spoon until well blended. Add lettuce. Toss. Serve with rye or pumpernickel bread. *Serves 4*

Favorite recipe from the **Roquefort Association, Inc.**

Fruit Salad Dressing

½ cup dairy sour cream
¼ cup **SKIPPY® Creamy** or **Chunk Style Peanut Butter**
¼ cup **KARO® Dark Corn Syrup**

Mix together sour cream, peanut butter and corn syrup. Serve over mixed fresh fruit salad. *Makes 1 cup*

Nature's Salad Dressing

½ cup salad oil
2 tablespoons **KIKKOMAN Soy Sauce**
2 teaspoons grated lemon rind
2 tablespoons lemon juice
2 tablespoons finely chopped parsley
1 tablespoon sesame seed, toasted
1 teaspoon honey

Combine all ingredients until well blended. Cover and refrigerate until ready to use. Mix well before serving. *Makes about ¾ cup*

Saucy Dressing

½ cup dairy sour cream
¼ cup mayonnaise or salad dressing
2 tablespoons **HEINZ 57 Sauce**
¼ teaspoon celery seed
¼ teaspoon salt
¼ teaspoon paprika
Dash hot pepper sauce

Blend ingredients. Cover; chill to blend flavors. Serve over lettuce wedges, tomato slices or Chef's salad. *Makes about 1 cup*

Hot Dan's Dressing

¼ cup **FRENCH'S® Prepared Mustard**
2 tablespoons sugar
2 tablespoons vinegar
2 tablespoons half-and-half or undiluted evaporated milk
¼ teaspoon salt

Combine all ingredients; beat with rotary beater until light and fluffy. Especially good in potato salad, coleslaw, and deviled eggs. *Makes ½ cup*

Danish French Dressing

⅓ cup red wine vinegar (or white wine vinegar or half
  wine vinegar and half lemon juice)
⅓ cup olive oil
⅓ cup salad oil
1 teaspoon salt
⅛ teaspoon white pepper
Dash or two of paprika and cayenne pepper
1 teaspoon sugar
1 clove garlic, pressed through garlic press
½ cup (2½ ounces) Danish Blue Cheese, crumbled

Combine all ingredients except cheese in a jar with a tight fitting
lid and shake well to blend. Add crumbled Danish Blue Cheese
and shake to blend.   *Makes 1½ cups*

Favorite recipe from the **Denmark Cheese Association**

Fluff®-Lemon Mayonnaise

Stir 1 Tbsp. lemon juice into ½ cup **MARSHMALLOW
FLUFF®**. Blend in ½ tsp. grated lemon peel. Add 1 cup mayonnaise, ¼ cup at a time, until smooth. Good on fresh-fruit salads.
                                                       Makes 1½ cups

Creamy Salad Dressing

1 cup dairy sour cream
½ cup mayonnaise
4 teaspoons **KIKKOMAN Soy Sauce**
1 teaspoon parsley flakes
¼ teaspoon onion powder
Dash paprika

Combine all ingredients until well blended. Let stand 10 minutes
before serving.   *Makes 1½ cups*

Calypso Salad Dressing

1 clove garlic, peeled
1 slice soft bread
1 can (1 lb.) stewed tomatoes
⅓ cup salad oil
2 tablespoons vinegar
½ teaspoon salt
¼ teaspoon pepper
1 teaspoon sugar
2 teaspoons **ANGOSTURA®** bitters

Cut garlic in three or four pieces and insert in bread. Let stand half
an hour and remove garlic. Mix tomatoes, oil, vinegar and seasonings. Add bread and beat until thoroughly mixed. Serve as dressing for mixed green salad.

BISON ✖®
House Dressing

1 pint **BISON Plain Yogurt**
¼ pint **BISON Sour Cream**
¼ pint **BISON Cottage Cheese**
¼ jar Hot-n-Spicy Mustard (to taste)
4 teaspoons white vinegar
Dash salt, garlic powder, onion salt

Just combine all ingredients and blend till smooth and creamy.
Chill and serve.

Vinaigrette Dressing

¾ cup **BERTOLLI® Olive Oil**
¼ cup **BERTOLLI® Red Wine Vinegar**
1 anchovy fillet, mashed (optional)
1 clove garlic, minced
½ teaspoon salt
¼ teaspoon pepper

Shake all ingredients in covered jar; refrigerate.

                                                       Makes 1 cup

REALEMON
Honeyed
Italian Dressing

¾ cup vegetable oil
½ cup **REALEMON® Reconstituted Lemon Juice**
¼ cup **BORDEN® Grated Parmesan and Romano
  Cheese**
¼ cup honey
½ teaspoon oregano leaves
¼ teaspoon salt
Dash pepper

In 1-pint jar with tight-fitting lid, combine ingredients; shake well.
Chill to blend flavors. Serve with tossed salad greens. Refrigerate.
                                                       Makes 1½ cups

Sealtest®
Orange Pineapple
Salad Dressing

¼ teaspoon sugar
¼ teaspoon grated orange peel
1 cup **SEALTEST® Cottage Cheese**
½ cup **SEALTEST® Sour Cream**
Dash salt
½ cup unsweetened pineapple juice
½ teaspoon lemon juice
6 tablespoons canned crushed pineapple and syrup

Mix sugar and orange peel; set aside. Sieve cottage cheese; fold in
sour cream. Add salt, pineapple and lemon juices, and crushed
pineapple; blend well. Fold in orange peel. Chill.   *2¼ cups*

SUE BEE HONEY
Piquant Salad Dressing

½ cup mayonnaise
½ cup fresh lemon juice
¼ cup **SUE BEE® Honey**
¼ teaspoon prepared mustard
Paprika
Extra seasonings if desired

Combine all ingredients in a jar or blender and mix well. Spoon over raw asparagus, cauliflower, tomatoes, cucumbers, or crisp lettuce wedges. *Makes 1¼ cups*

Low Calorie Dressing

1 can (10 oz.) **SNAP-E-TOM® Tomato Cocktail**
6 tablespoons frozen concentrated orange juice
1 tablespoon lemon juice
1 teaspoon onion powder
½ teaspoon garlic powder
½ teaspoon celery salt
Salt to taste

Combine all ingredients and stir until well blended. Chill until ready to serve. *Makes about 1½ cups*

wesson OIL
Wesson® 2-Minute Basic Mayonnaise

1 egg
¼ tsp. salt
2 Tbsp. lemon juice
1 cup **WESSON® Oil**

Combine egg, salt, lemon juice and ¼ cup **WESSON®** in blender container. Blend together until mixture begins to thicken. Blend in *remaining* ¾ cup **WESSON®**, pouring in a thin stream until mixture is thick and smooth, about 2 minutes. Allow slightly longer beating time for rotary or electric beater. *Makes about 1 cup*

Note: For best results have all ingredients at room temperature.

DANNON YOGURT
Yogurt "Mayonnaise"

1 cup **DANNON® Plain Yogurt**
2 Tbsp. butter
4 Tbsp. flour
1 cup milk
1 egg yolk
2 Tbsp. lemon juice
½ tsp. dry mustard
½ tsp. salt

Melt the butter in a skillet and stir in flour. Add milk all at once and stir over medium heat until thick. Remove from heat and beat in egg yolk, lemon juice, mustard and salt. Stir in yogurt & cool. *Makes approximately 2 cups*

Family French Dressing

Combine ½ cup **HEINZ Tomato Ketchup**, ½ cup salad oil, ¼ cup **HEINZ Apple Cider Vinegar**, 2 teaspoons confectioners' sugar, 1 clove garlic, split, ¼ teaspoon salt and dash pepper; shake vigorously. Chill to blend flavors. Remove garlic; shake again before serving. *Makes 1¼ cups*

Blue Fox French Dressing

5 oz. **STAR Olive Oil**
3 oz. **STAR Red Wine Vinegar**
1 tsp. chopped chives or chopped green onions
1 tsp. chopped parsley
Salt and pepper to taste

Combine all ingredients in a jar. Shake well before using.

DANNON YOGURT
Cucumber Parsley Dressing

1 cup mayonnaise
1 cup pared, seeded, chopped cucumber
2 tablespoons finely chopped parsley
1 clove garlic, minced
½ teaspoon salt
⅛ teaspoon ground black pepper
1 cup **DANNON® Plain Yogurt**

Stir together first 6 ingredients. Fold in yogurt. Chill. *Makes 2⅔ cups*

Tangy Coconut Salad Dressing for Fruit, Ham or Chicken Salads

½ cup corn oil
½ cup **COCO CASA™ Cream of Coconut**
1 can (6 ozs.) frozen concentrated orange juice, thawed and undiluted
¼ tsp. curry powder
½ tsp. salt

In a bowl, combine all ingredients and beat until smooth and thick. Chill until ready to serve. Beat again and toss with salad when ready to serve. *Makes 1¾ cups*

Strawberry-Walnut Dressing

Soften 1 package (3 ounces) cream cheese. Beat in until smooth ½ cup halved fresh strawberries, 1½ tablespoons granulated sugar, 2 tablespoons lemon juice, 1/16 teaspoon salt and ¼ cup finely chopped, toasted **DIAMOND® Walnuts**. Serve on a mixture of 1 can (8¼ ounces) pineapple chunks, 1 cup halved pitted prunes and 2 cups assorted sliced or diced fresh fruits. *Makes 4 servings*

Acknowledgments

The Editors of CONSUMER GUIDE® wish to thank the companies and organizations listed for use of their recipes and artwork. For further information contact the following:

Alaska Seafood Mktg. Inst.—Pacific Kitchen
300 Elliott Ave. W.
Seattle, WA 98119

Amber Brand Deviled Smithfield Ham
The Smithfield Ham and Products Co.
Smithfield, VA 23430

American Beauty®, *see* Pillsbury Co., The

American Egg Board
1460 Renaissance
Park Ridge, IL 60068

Angostura®—A-W Brands, Inc.
Carteret, NJ 07008

Armour and Company
Phoenix, AZ 85077

Atalanta/Krakus/Polka—Atalanta Corp.
17 Varick St.
New York, NY 10013

B&B Liqueur, *see* Wile, Julius

BinB®, *see* Clorox Co., The

Bac*Os, *see* General Mills, Inc.

Banquet Foods Corp.
Ballwin, MO 63011

Bertolli U.S.A.
P.O. Box 931
So. San Francisco, CA 94080

Best Foods
Englewood Cliffs, NJ 07632

Betty Crocker®, *see* General Mills, Inc.

Bison Foods Co., Inc.
196 Scott St.
Buffalo, NY 14204

Blue Diamond®—Calif. Almond Growers Exch.
P.O. Box 1768
Sacramento, CA 95808

Blue Ribbon®—Continental Nut Co.
Chico, CA 95927

Boggs®, *see* Heublin/Spirits Group

Booth Fisheries Corp.
2 North Riverside Plaza
Chicago, IL 60606

Borden Inc.
180 E. Broad St.
Columbus, OH 43215

Bordo Products Company
2825 Sheffield Ave.
Chicago, IL 60657

Breakstone's®, *see* Kraft, Inc.—Dairy Group

Breyers®, *see* Kraft, Inc.—Dairy Group

Brownberry
Oconomowoc, WI 53066

Bud of California®, *see* Castle & Cooke

Buddig, Carl, & Co.
11914 S. Peoria St.
Chicago, IL 60643

Bumble Bee®, *see* Castle & Cooke

Butter Buds®, *see* Cumberland Packing

Butterball®—Swift & Co.
Oak Brook, IL 60521

Calavo Growers of California
Box 3486, Terminal Annex
Los Angeles, CA 90051

California Apricot Advisory Board
Walnut Creek, CA 94595

California Avocado Commission
Irvine, CA 92714

California Brandy Advisory Board
426 Pacific Avenue
San Francisco, CA 94133

California Iceberg Lettuce Commission
P.O. Box 3354
Monterey, CA 93940

Campbell Soup Co.
Camden, NJ 08101

Cape Granny Smith Apples
Dudley, Anderson, Yutzy
40 W. 57th St.
New York, NY 10019

Castle & Cooke Foods
50 California St.
San Francisco, CA 94119

Cheez-It®—Sunshine Biscuits, Inc.
245 Park Ave.
New York, NY 10017

Cheez-Ola®, *see* Fisher Cheese Co.

Chef Boy-Ar-Dee®—American Home Foods
685 Third Ave.
New York, NY 10017

Chicken of the Sea®—Ralston Purina Co.
St. Louis, MO 63188

Chieftan Wild Rice Co.
Hayward, WI 54843

Chiquita Brands, Inc.
Montvale, NJ 07645

Christian Brothers®, The—Fromm and Sichel, Inc.
San Francisco, CA 94120

Claussen, *see* Oscar Mayer Foods Corp.

Clorox Co., The
Oakland, CA 94623

Coca-Cola Co., The
P. O. Drawer 1734
Atlanta, GA 30301

Coco Casa™, *see* Holland House Brands

Cookin' Good™—Showell Farms, Inc.
P.O. Box 158
Showell, MD 21862-0158

Count Down®, *see* Fisher Cheese Co.

Creamette Co., The
Minneapolis, MN 55401

Crisco®, *see* Procter & Gamble Co.

Cumberland Packing Corp.
2 Cumberland St.
Brooklyn, NY 11205

Dannon Co., The
22-11 38th Ave.
Long Island City, NY 11101

Darigold—Consolidated Dairy Products
635 Elliott Ave. W.
Seattle, WA 98109

Del Monte Corp.
P. O. Box 3575
San Francisco, CA 94119

Deming's, *see* Peter Pan Seafoods

Denmark Cheese Assn.
4415 W. Harrison
Hillside, IL 60163

Diamond®, *see* Sun-Diamond Growers

Diet Shasta®—Shasta Beverages
Hayward, CA 94545

Dole®, *see* Castle & Cooke Foods

Domino®—Amstar Corp.
1251 Avenue of the Americas
New York, NY 10020

Doritos®—Frito-Lay, Inc.
Dallas, TX 75235

Dorman, N., & Co.
Syosett, NY 11791

Double Q, *see* Peter Pan Seafoods

Drambuie®—Taylor, W.A., & Co.
825 South Bayshore Dr.
Miami, FL 33131

Dry Sack®, *see* Wile, Julius

Dubonnet®—Schenley Affiliated Brands
888 Seventh Ave.
New York, NY 10106

Durkee Foods—Div. of SCM Corp.
Strongsville, OH 44136

Estee Corp., The
Parsippany, NJ 07054

Farm-Raised Catfish—Catfish Farmers of America
P.O. Box 34
Jackson, MS 39205

Featherweight®—Chicago Dietetic Supply, Inc.
La Grange, IL 60525

Figaro Co., The
111 Manufacturing St.
Dallas, TX 75207

Filippo Berio—Berio Importing Corp.
109 Montgomery Ave.
Scarsdale, NJ 10583

Finlandia Cheese, *see* Atalanta Corp.

Fireside—Doumak Illinois, Inc.
Elk Grove Village, IL 60007

Fisher Cheese Co.
Wapakoneta, OH 45895

Florida Dept. of Natural Resources
3900 Commonwealth Blvd.
Tallahassee, FL 32303

Florida Lime Administrative Committee
700 Barksdale Rd.
Newark, DE 19711

Franco American, *see* Campbell Soup Co.

French, R. T., Co.
Rochester, NY 14609

Gallo Salame
250 Brannan St.
San Francisco, CA 94107

General Foods
White Plains, NY 10625

General Mills, Inc.
Minneapolis, MN 55440

Gerber Products Co.
Fremont, MI 49412

Gibson Wine Co.
Elk Grove, CA 95624

Gillnettersbest, *see* Peter Pan

Good Seasons®, *see* General Foods

Green Giant®, *see* Pillsbury Co., The

Grey Poupon®, *see* Heublein/Spirits Group

Hamburger Helper®, *see* General Mills

Heinz U.S.A.
Pittsburgh, PA 15212

Hellmann's®, *see* Best Foods

Herb-Ox®—The Pure Food Co.
Mamaroneck, NY 10543

Heublein Inc.—Grocery Products
Farmington, CT 06032

Heublein/Spirits Group
330 New Park Ave.
Hartford, CT 06101

Hidden Valley Original Ranch®, *see* Clorox Co., The

Hiram Walker Inc.
P. O. Box 33006
Detroit, MI 48232

Holland House Brands Co.
1125 Pleasant View Terrace
Ridgefield, NJ 07657

Hormel, Geo. A., & Co.
Austin, MN 55912

Humpty Dumpty, *see* Peter Pan Seafoods

Imperial Sugar Co.
P. O. Box 50129
Dallas, TX 75250

Irish Mist®, *see* Heublein/Spirits Group

Jell-O®, *see* General Foods

Jennie-O Brand Turkey Meat
Willmar, MN 56201

Jif®, *see* Procter & Gamble Co.

Kahn's and Co.
3241 Spring Grove Ave.
Cincinnati, OH 45225

Karo®, *see* Best Foods

Kellogg Co.
Battle Creek, MI 49016

Kikkoman International, Inc.
50 California St.
San Francisco, CA 94111

King Oscar Fine Foods
Millburn, NJ 07041

Knox®, *see* Lipton, Thomas J., Inc.

Kool-Aid®, *see* General Foods

Kraft, Inc.
Glenview, IL 60025

Kraft, Inc.—Dairy Group
P.O. Box 7830
Philadelphia, PA 19101

Krakus, *see* Atalanta Corp.

Kretschmer—International Multifoods
Eighth & Marquette
Minneapolis, MN 55402

La Choy Food Products
Archbold, OH 43502

Le Sueur®, *see* Pillsbury Co., The

Lea & Perrins, Inc.
Fair Lawn, NJ 07410

Leafy Greens Council
503 S. Oak Park Ave.
Oak Park, IL 60304

Libby, McNeill & Libby, Inc.
200 S. Michigan Ave.
Chicago, IL 60604

Lindsay International Inc.
Visalia, CA 93277

Lipton, Thomas J., Inc.
Englewood Cliffs, NJ 07632

Louisiana Brand—Robinson Canning Co.
Westwego, LA 70094

Lucky Leaf—Knouse Foods Cooperative
Peach Glen, PA 17036

Marshmallow Fluff—Durkee-Mower, Inc.
Lynn, MA 01903

Mazola®, *see* Best Foods

McCormick & Co., Inc.
414 Light St.
Baltimore, MD 21202

Meadow Gold Dairies
1526 S. State St.
Chicago, IL 60605

Michigan Apple Committee
2726 E. Michigan Ave.
Lansing, MI 48912

Migliore®—Scheps Cheese
Haledon, NJ 07538

Milnot Co.
P. O. Box 190
Litchfield, IL 62056

Minute Maid®—The Coca-Cola Co.
P.O. Box 2079
Houston, TX 77001

Miracle Whip, *see* Kraft, Inc.

Mr. & Mrs. "T"
20321 S. Susana Rd.
Compton, CA 90221

Mueller, C. F., Co.
180 Baldwin Ave.
Jersey City, NJ 07306

Nabisco Brands, Inc.
625 Madison Ave.
New York, NY 10022

Nalley's Fine Foods Div.
3303 S. 35th
Tacoma, WA 98411

National Hot Dog & Sausage Council
400 W. Madison
Chicago, IL 60606

National Marine Fisheries Service
Washington, DC 20235

Old London®, see Borden Inc.

Ore-Ida Foods, Inc.
Boise, ID 83707

Ortega®, see Heublein Inc.—Grocery
Products

Oscar Mayer Foods Corp.
P.O. Box 7188
Madison, WI 53707

P&R, see San-Giorgio-Skinner, Inc.

Pepperidge Farm, Inc.
Norwalk, CT 06856

Pet, Inc.
St. Louis, MO 63166

Peter Pan Seafoods, Inc.
Dexter Horton Bldg.
Seattle, WA 98104

Pickle Packers International
St. Charles, IL 60174

Pillsbury Co., The
Minneapolis, MN 55402

Polka, see Atalanta Corp.

Pompeian, Inc.
4201 Pulaski Hwy.
Baltimore, MD 21224

Procter & Gamble Co.
Cincinnati, OH 45202

Progresso Quality Foods
Rochelle Park, NJ 07662

Puritan®, see Procter & Gamble Co.

Ragu®—Chesebrough Pond's Inc.
Trumbull, CT 06611

Rath Packing Co.
Waterloo, IA 50704

ReaLemon®, see Borden Inc.

Regina®, see Heublein/Spirits Group

Romanoff®—Iroquois Grocery Products
111 High Ridge Rd.
Stamford, CT 06902

Roni-Mac®, see Pillsbury Co., The

Ronzoni Macaroni Co., Inc.
50-02 Northern Blvd.
Long Island City, NY 11101

Roquefort Association, Inc.
41 E. 42nd St.
New York, NY 10017

S&W Fine Foods, Inc.
San Mateo, CA 94402

Salad Crispins®, see Clorox, Co., The

San Giorgio-Skinner, Inc.
Hershey, PA 17033

Sargento Cheese Co.
Plymouth, WI 53073

Schilling®, see McCormick & Co., Inc.

Sealtest®, see Kraft, Inc.—Dairy Group

Shoal Lake Wild Rice Ltd.
Keewatin, Ont., Canada POX 1CO

Skippy®, see Best Foods

Snack Mate, see Nabisco Brands, Inc.

Snap-E-Tom®, see Heublein Inc.—Grocery
Products

Solo®—Sokol and Co.
Countryside, IL 60525

Southern Comfort Corp.
1220 N. Price Rd.
St. Louis, MO 63132

Star—A. Giurlani & Bro., Inc.
P.O. Box 1315
Sunnyvale, CA 94086

Star-Kist Foods, Inc.
Terminal Island, CA 90731

Stokely-Van Camp, Inc.
Indianapolis, IN 46206

Success®—Rivinia Foods Inc.
P.O. Box 2636
Houston, TX 77001

Sue Bee®—Sioux Honey Assn.
Sioux City, IA 51102

Sun-Diamond Growers of California
San Ramon, CA 94583

Sun-Maid®, see Sun-Diamond Growers

Sun World, Inc.
5544 California Ave.
Bakersfield, CA 93309

Sunkist Growers, Inc.
Van Nuys, CA 93309

Sunshine Biscuits, Inc.
245 Park Ave.
New York, NY 10017

Swanson, see Campbell Soup Co.

Sweet 'N Low®, see Cumberland Packing

Sweetlite™—Batterlite Whitlock Inc.
P.O. Box 259
Springfield, IL 62705

Swift & Co.
Oak Brook, IL 60521

Tabasco®—McIlhenny Co.
Avery Island, LA 70513

Taylor Packing Co., John W.
Hallwood, VA 23359

Texasweet Citrus Advertising, Inc.
McAllen, TX 78501

Thank You®—Michigan Fruit Canners
Benton Harbor, MI 49022

Tuna Research Foundation, Inc.
1101 17th St. N.W.
Washington, DC 20036

Two Fingers®, see Hiram Walker Inc.

Uncle Ben's Foods
Houston, TX 77001

Underwood, Wm., Co.
Westwood, MA 02090

Valio, see Atalanta Corp.

Van De Kamp's Frozen Foods
13100 Arctic Circle
Santa Fe Springs, CA 90670

Veg-All®—The Larsen Co.
520 N. Broadway
Green Bay, WI 54305

Vienna Sausage Mfg. Co.
2501 N. Damen Ave.
Chicago, IL 60647

Wakefield®—Pacific Pearl Seafoods
1450 114th Ave. S.E.
Bellevue, WA 98004

Wesson®—Hunt-Wesson Kitchen
1645 W. Valencia Dr.
Fullerton, CA 92634

Wile, Julius, Sons & Co., Inc.
Lake Success, NY 11042

Wilson Foods Corp.
Oklahoma City, OK 73105

Wish-Bone®, see Lipton, Thomas, J.

Wolf Brand Products
2929 Carlisle St.
Dallas, TX 75204

Wyler's®, see Borden Inc.

Index